Carol A. W9-ADO-025

Continuous Improvement
in the
Primary Classroom

Also Available from ASQ Quality Press

Improving Student Learning: Applying Deming's Quality Principles in Classrooms
Lee Jenkins

Continuous Improvement in the Science Classroom
Jeffrey Burgard

Thinking Tools for Kids: An Activity Book for Classroom Learning
Barbara A. Cleary, Ph.D. and Sally J. Duncan

Futuring Tools for Strategic Quality Planning in Education
William F. Alexander and Richard W. Serfass

Quality Team Learning for Schools: A Principal's Perspective
James E. Abbott

The New Philosophy for K–12 Education: A Deming Framework for Transforming America's Schools
James F. Leonard

Creating Dynamic Teaching Teams in Schools
K. Mark Kevesdy and Tracy A. Burich, with contributions from Kelly A. Spier

Success Through Quality: Support Guide for the Journey to Continuous Improvement
Timothy J. Clark

To request a complimentary catalog of ASQ Quality Press publications, call 800-248-1946, or visit our Web site at qualitypress.asq.org.

Continuous Improvement in the Primary Classroom

Language Arts, Grades K–3

Karen R. Fauss

ASQ Quality Press
Milwaukee, Wisconsin

Continuous Improvement in the Primary Classroom: Language Arts, Grades K–3
Karen R. Fauss

Library of Congress Cataloging-in-Publication Data

Fauss, Karen R., 1955–
    Continuous improvement in the primary classroom : language arts,
    grades K–3 / Karen R. Fauss.
        p. cm.
    Includes bibliographical references and index.
    ISBN 0-87389-429-4 (alk. paper)
    1. Language arts (Primary)—United States. I. Title.
LD1528.F38 2000
372.6 21—dc21   99-044825
                                                              CIP

© 2000 by ASQ

All rights reserved. No part of this book may be reproduced in any form or by any means, electronic, mechanical, photocopying, recording, or otherwise, without the prior written permission of the publisher.

10 9 8 7 6 5 4 3 2 1

ISBN 0-87389-429-4

Acquisitions Editor: Ken Zielske

Project Editor: Annemieke Koudstaal

Production Administrator: Shawn Dohogne

ASQ Mission: The American Society for Quality advances individual and organizational performance excellence worldwide by providing opportunities for learning, quality improvement, and knowledge exchange.

Attention: Bookstores, Wholesalers, Schools and Corporations:
ASQ Quality Press books, videotapes, audiotapes, and software are available at quantity discounts with bulk purchases for business, educational, or instructional use. For information, please contact ASQ Quality Press at 800-248-1946, or write to ASQ Quality Press, P.O. Box 3005, Milwaukee, WI 53201-3005.

To place orders or to request a free copy of the ASQ Quality Press Publications Catalog, including ASQ membership information, call 800-248-1946. Visit our Web site at www.asq.org or qualitypress.asq.org.

Printed in the United States of America

∞ Printed on acid-free paper

American Society for Quality

ASQ

Quality Press
611 East Wisconsin Avenue
Milwaukee, Wisconsin 53202
Call toll free 800-248-1946
www.asq.org
qualitypress.asq.org
standardsgroup.asq.org

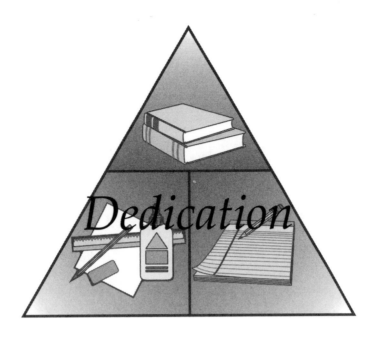

I will be forever grateful to my husband, Richard, for his unconditional love and tenacious support. This book is dedicated to him.

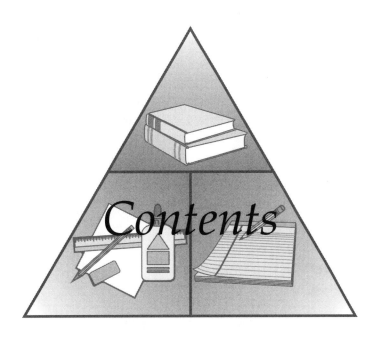

Contents

List of Figures

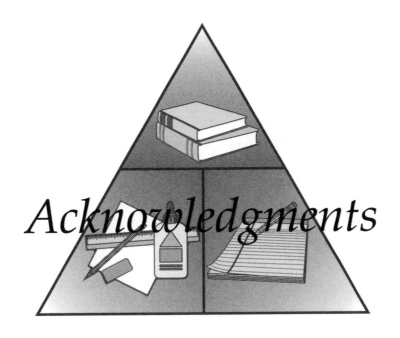

Acknowledgments

"When Quality becomes a way of life, we rise to a state of being characterized by what Deming called a natural 'pride and joy' in the processes and products of our lives through a yearning for learning that is lifelong, life-wide, and life-deep. This is a journey without end, an invitation to participate in a lifelong adventure to seek out the very best that life has to offer!"

JOHN JAY BONSTINGL[1]

I am deeply grateful to all my teachers—those of both my childhood years and my adulthood—who have invested their lives in my continuous improvement journey.

I am very blessed to have been born into a very supportive, loving, immediate and extended family. Their encouragement never ceases.

My special appreciation is extended to two masters, Dr. Lee Jenkins and his wife Sandy, for investing their wealth of wisdom in me when I embarked on a new career as a fledgling teacher in my late thirties. They still continue to mentor me.

There are many other masters who have greatly enhanced my professional career through their books, conference sessions, and teacher inservices, and continue to influence my thinking as I reread and study their profound knowledge. I treasure the memories of meeting and speaking with Dr. William Glasser, Margaret Byrnes, Myron Tribus, Franklin Schargel, John Jay Bonstingl, Michael Schmoker, Peggy McLean, Mary Laycock, and Evelyn Neufeld.

I consider it an honor to be employed as a teacher in Enterprise School District. Special thanks is given to my administrators for their support and encouragement: Dr. Lee Jenkins, Nancy Schultz, Tom Armelino, Bill Rich, Glen Eaton, and Jack Greenfield. I am also indebted to many professional colleagues for all they have taught me: Jeff Burgard, Shelly Carson, Carolyn Ayres Mercer, Kimi Kinoshita, Lynda Peddy, Brien McCall, Dan and Judy Flores, Kristi Ostrom, Kristin Nobles, Harley North, Mark and Kathy Klinesteker, Dennis Mitchell, Karen Provence, and countless others around the nation.

It is a privilege to be part of the wonderful team of educators at Boulder Creek School. I want to express gratitude to the teachers of my supply, kindergarten teaching partners Nancy Cavagnaro and Kristin Brown, for working weekly with my second-grade students; and to my first-grade teaching partners, Marc Shelby and Dana Kamla, for allowing my second-grade students to read and share completed projects with their first-grade students. All four teachers have offered so much support for my program. I have enjoyed collaborating with past and present second-grade teammates: Debbie Spiess, Debbie Lungi, Kathryn McCoach, Shere DePaoli, Suzan Harvey, Kaoma Birkland, Bryan White, and Dale McMahon. It has been an honor to have worked next door to Dale McMahon for the past six years. Many ideas in this book are the result of his continuous mentorship, for which I am especially grateful.

I am also grateful to my customers, third-grade colleagues Geri Bramwell, Shere DePaoli, and Colleen Silva, for working with my students in writing and social studies. They have offered many constructive suggestions for continuous improvement in my second-grade program. My fourth- and fifth-grade colleagues, Erlee Dawn Eoff, Carol Hodge, Amy Coots, and Rich Bourne, have allowed their students to mentor my second-grade students in reading and math. I am thankful for their support. Special thanks is offered to Ginger Geiger and some of her students from Central Valley High School for engaging in writing projects with my second-grade students. I am very grateful for all the tireless hours she invested in my program as a parent volunteer. I sincerely appreciate all my past and present students and their parents. They have taught me many valuable lessons.

Notes

1. John Jay Bonstingl, _Schools of Quality_ (Alexandria, VA: ASCD, 1996), 67–68.

Foreword

by Lee Jenkins

The books in the ASQ Continuous Improvement Series are written for teachers who possess both the utmost respect for their students and a desire to improve student learning. Teachers are often frustrated because the tools society provides for student improvement do not honor their respect for students.

Four currently popular methods for improving student learning are these: (1) add more fear to the lives of students; (2) bribe students with incentives to do better or more work; (3) set up false competition between students; and (4) purchase a new program and demand its use.

There are, however, thousands of teachers who love and respect their students and recognize that fear, bribery, false competition, and my-way-or-the-highway approaches don't work. At best they achieve short-term results. The books in the ASQ Continuous Improvement Series, by Fauss, Burgard, Carson, and Ayres Mercer, are written from the hearts of teachers who possess the two criteria mentioned in the first paragraph. They love and respect their students while maintaining an intense desire to improve their students' learning.

These teachers clearly describe their experiences with a fifth option: studying and using data for continual improvements. They document the systems their classrooms use to collect weekly data, as well as the process of making curricular decisions based upon their data. The data is from students' long-term memories. There is no place for cramming and short-term memory. The teachers and their students, functioning as a team, can and do plan their improvements. They know within a few weeks if the instructional plans are working or not. No longer must these teachers wait until July to see results.

Readers will enjoy these teachers' experiences and stories, but most of all they will learn exactly how to restructure the management of their classroom learning systems toward significant improvement.

Each of the four authors in the ASQ Continuous Improvement Series brings a unique view of quality processes into his or her classroom.

Fauss: In the culture of education, teachers call themselves lucky when they have an exceptionally bright class. The unstated inference is that the next year will return to normal. What happens, however, when a teacher is determined to prove that every year will end with better results than the previous year? After a year or two, this becomes intense, because the easy ideas are used up. Fauss incorporates dynamic language arts methods with the tools for continuous improvement. Talent and passion will transfer from her pen to the minds and hearts of readers.

Burgard: It is clear that Burgard sees the application of quality principles through the eyes of a scientist. He changed the English department's rubric into a dichotomous key, and he analyzed student writing errors like a chemist. Further, he knows science is not science unless it can be replicated. This means students must have precise knowledge of definitions and clear understanding of scientific processes. Both information and knowledge are essential; there's no room for an educational pendulum in Burgard's thinking.

Carson: Most surveys of school attitude document that history/social science is the most hated of school subjects. Readers of Carson's book will easily see, however, why history is her students' favorite subject. Not only are they loving to learn the facts of history, they are thinking like historians. She pushes student involvement in planning further than I've ever seen—even including scheduling lessons and assignments. This is not just the Carson show—it's better.

Ayres Mercer: This book combines the principles of quality with research taken from the Third International Math and Science Study (TIMSS). As a part of this study, videos were made that demonstrate Japanese methods of teaching mathematics. Ayres Mercer has combined these Japanese methods with principles of quality. Her work is truly unique in the world of mathematics education. Further, she documents her students' growth in mathematics concepts weekly, and their attitude toward mathematics monthly. Her formula for success is this:

mathematics concepts + mathematics problem solving + great attitudes + the data to prove each is occurring = great school mathematics

The poorer an idea, the more age specific it is; the better the idea, the wider the age span it has. Even though these four teachers each teach a particular grade and relate stories about a particular age group, audiences from kindergarten through college may benefit from their provocative lessons.

"Some people come into our lives and quickly go. Some stay for a while and leave footprints on our heart and we are never, ever the same."[1]

This book describes one primary teacher's journey in continuous improvement, and her effort to use quality principles and concepts to improve her classroom system. I am that teacher. During the last several years I've read, learned, experimented with, and applied the theories and practices of many masters in quality theory, especially W. Edwards Deming, the father of the field. All the books I read are listed in the reference section of the book. There are many resources that explain Deming's theory of profound knowledge in detail. Other authors have researched, practiced, and applied quality tools in many different classroom settings. The pages of this book were written from a learner's perspective, referring often to the masters who greatly influence my thinking. I continue to learn from them, and I recommend the reader to these same sources of wisdom. As Dr. Deming said, "Learn from the masters; they are few."[2]

Recently a teacher asked me after my presentation at a conference, "How did you find out about Deming's theories?" It began when I had the privilege of meeting and learning from Dr. William Glasser during a teacher training session in 1992. I was inspired to read his book *The Quality School*. He also gave me a draft copy of *The Quality School Teacher*, not yet published at that time. That same year, I encountered Margaret Byrnes at another conference. After eagerly reading her *The Quality Teacher, Implementing Total Quality Management in the Classroom* (also published in 1992) at least twice, I realized I had met two masters that year. Thus I embarked on a new path. In his poem "The Road Not Taken,"[3] Robert Frost captures the way I view the beginning of my quality journey:

Two roads diverged in a wood, and I—
I took the one less traveled by,
And that has made all the difference.

Chapter 1 explains how to view a classroom as a system, with a description of each component. Subsequent chapters explain more in-depth, systemic thinking in curricular areas (with a focus on language arts) and how quality tools are applied to improve student learning. Feedback is gathered from customers: current students, former students, parents, and teaching colleagues. My students are teamed up with students from other grade levels in creative learning experiences.

The purpose of this book is not to *teach* quality tools, but to show the *usefulness* of the tools to maintain enthusiasm while increasing student learning. There are many excellent books available for that purpose in the bibliography. Decisions are made, based upon data or facts gathered from my students, to help manage the learning in my classroom. Each year my students and I work through continuous improvement processes. Data from the last five years will be shared to demonstrate how each successive class has outperformed the previous class.

Most of the graphs in the book were created using Class Action software. More information about this program is listed in Appendix B. To date, I am aware of no other program designed from this perspective for classroom use. Everything I have produced with the software can be done by hand, plotting data points onto a piece of grid paper. There are teachers and students who successfully collect and plot the data by hand in one subject. I started collecting data in spelling. Each year I collected data in an additional subject area. The software makes data collection in spelling, math, reading fluency, and science easily manageable. Other yearly comparative graphs in the manuscript were made using Cricket Graph™ and Excel™. Please keep in mind as you read the book that the graphs display data collected both from individual students and from whole classes. Data help to inform teacher instruction, as well as to communicate progress to students and parents. As one reader commented, "the book got me excited about data collection and enthused about improving myself as a teacher!"

My purpose in writing this book is to inspire and encourage you along your journey in quality. As you read, I hope you sense the enthusiasm in my classroom and understand that you, too, can enhance your own students' lives as your classroom continuously improves using Dr. Deming's quality principles. John Jay Bonstingl offers this advice: "Make your journey to Total Quality a slow and steady process. The Quality transformation takes time. . . . Approach your Total Quality transformation with patience, forgiveness, and a helping hand. Total Quality is a journey, not a destination."[4] A journey begins with a single step. . . .

Notes

1. Jack Canfield and Mark Victor Hansen, *A 3rd Serving of Chicken Soup for the Soul* (Deerfield Beach, FL: Health Communications, 1996), 134.
2. Lee Jenkins, *Improving Student Learning* (Milwaukee, WI: ASQ Quality Press, 1997), p. xix.
3. Robert Frost, "The Road Not Taken," 1915.
4. John Jay Bonstingl, *Schools of Quality* (Alexandria, VA: Association for Supervision and Curriculum Development, 1996), 55.

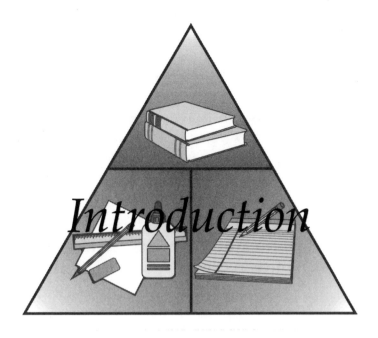

Introduction

In 1950, after the end of World War II, General Douglas MacArthur's office invited William Edwards Deming to come to Japan and give a series of lectures on statistical quality control. Dr. Deming taught them how to use the PDSA cycle (see chapter 2) to constantly improve quality, "which he had done earlier for audiences in the United States."[1] Later, concluding his speech at a dinner given for some assembled industrial leaders, Dr. Deming pledged that "if they followed his advice and made quality their number one priority, consumers worldwide would be clamoring for Japanese products within five years. Even Deming himself privately thought his estimate optimistic. And yet, amazingly, it took only four years for his prophesy to begin to be realized."[2] In 1999, I am convinced that "quality" is still synonymous with products produced in Japan.

Periodically review the following key elements of Dr. Deming's epistemologic thinking, applied to education, as you read the rest of the book.

Deming's Key Elements

1. Information is about the past; knowledge is necessary to create a better future.

2. Learn from the masters; they are few.

3. Only one example contrary to a theory is necessary to cause revision of the theory.

4. Learning comes from testing theories. "Without theory there is no learning, and thus no improvement—only motion."

5. Knowledge is necessary to better predict the future.

6. The responsibility of leaders is to create more leaders.

7. Experience alone gives no knowledge.[3]

Notes

1. John Jay Bonstingl, *Schools of Quality* (Alexandria, VA: ASCD, 1996), 12.
2. Ibid., 14.
3. Lee Jenkins, *Improving Student Learning* (Milwaukee, WI: ASQ Quality Press, 1997), 24.

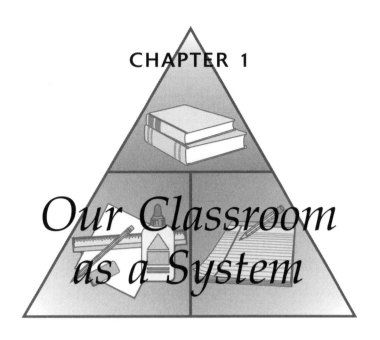

CHAPTER 1

Our Classroom as a System

"A quality system is built on a foundation of fact."

STEVEN GEORGE[1]

The purpose of chapter 1 is to introduce the classroom system as a whole, so that the reader may see all of its components (Figure 1.1). Examples and explanations of the components will be given so you can begin to study your own system and use quality tools to involve students in the improvement process. All seven components of the system can be glued together with customized information, laminated, and placed on a wall in the classroom as a visual reminder.

After reviewing the components, you are probably wondering why there is a need for a classroom system. In the past, when educators talked about classroom management, they referred only to the management of behavior. That approach did not necessarily refer to management of learning and enthusiasm in a classroom. Dr. W. Edwards Deming provided educators with the statistical means to manage learning. He told a story about a car which illustrates this

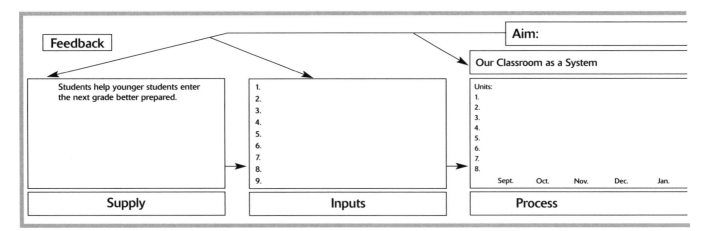

Figure 1.1. The seven elements of the classroom system.

point. "If you take the best engine in the world, plus the best transmission, plus the best steering, etc. and put all of the pieces together, you have not one car that will run."[2] The story was applied to education by Dr. Lee Jenkins: "It is possible to have nice kids, smart teacher, good parents, nice building, good principal and not have a classroom that works. Very small pieces can be missing in a car and it won't start. If elements of a classroom system are missing, the classroom won't function well."[3] Throughout this book I will describe in detail how Deming's management theories are used to manage learning and maintain enthusiasm in my primary classroom.

My classroom system has shown weekly improvement, as evidenced by data I collect, graph, and analyze from student learning. The process data enable me to improve my instruction by making informed decisions. The previous week's cumulative class data are shared with the students in the form of a class scatter diagram, histogram, or line graph. "By sharing the feedback, the teacher and students plan together different instructional strategies so that they will learn more successfully."[4]

The whole reason for gathering process data is to gain insight into how to bring about learning improvement. Process data are different than results data in that the students, parents, and teacher use process data in an ongoing process of bringing about improvement. Results data, on the other hand, are gathered at the end of a school year. The results are used to improve the next year's classroom system.

"When the goal is improvement, the teacher believes that the person with the major responsibility for student success is the teacher."[5] I am a teacher with a passion for improved student learning, but at the same time I cannot allow students to lose their enthusiasm for learning. They entered kindergarten with all the enthusiasm they will ever need. As a classroom of learners, we work together to find and eliminate the negatives that squelch enthusiasm.

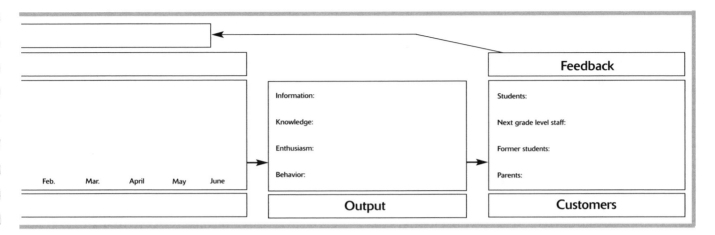

Figure 1.1. Continued.

Students must leave my classroom with the same joy for learning they had when they began kindergarten.

Deming's Aim for Education

Dr. Deming offered the following aim for education in January of 1992 at the American Association of School Administrators Conference in Washington D.C.: "Increase the positives and decrease the negatives so that all students keep their yearning for learning."[6] Throughout the year, my job as a primary grade teacher is to figure out which positives help maintain the joy in my classroom system, and then to celebrate them often. Another challenge is to find creative ways to spread those positives to other classrooms at my school site.

Learning Celebrations

Students enter my classroom with their intrinsic motivation. I do not need to bribe them with extrinsic rewards to bring about learning. This does not mean, however, that we don't celebrate. Celebrations plus continual feedback help me "increase the positives and decrease the negatives."[7]

The parent-teacher conference can be a time of celebration when reviewing a student's progress. Another teacher in our district suggested I include both the child and the parents at the conference, which I now do every year. We, as a team, brainstorm solutions to problems. I believe the child will take more ownership of the solution if he or she is included in the process. If there are any sensitive issues that must be discussed privately with the parents, I save those for the end of the conference, while the student plays a learning game in another part of the classroom or listens to a book on tape with headphones.

One time we celebrate our learning successes is at the beginning of the year, with our parents and students from other grades. Kindergarten and first-grade students are invited to watch the dress rehearsal of our annual Ant, Butterfly, Bee Tea performance. Forty second-grade students sing choreographed songs and recite poems accompanied with sign language and drama. The next day our adjacent classrooms are organized as insect museums. Second-grade students act as museum docents, teaching and sharing their completed work with younger students for twenty minute intervals. (Many of these students will be the supply for my classroom in the future.) When the afternoon performance for our parents concludes in the multi-purpose room, the parents enjoy the insect museums in the classrooms. The children share completed projects produced during the first nine weeks of school. After dessert and tea, all the insect museum artifacts are taken home.

Many benefits result from this celebration. The other second-grade teacher and I receive many positive comments about how well the students perform together. All the rehearsals help fuse the separate classrooms into a second-grade team. Our high expectations for student achievement are established during the celebration. The graphed process data I gather during this unit, reviewing and previewing insect facts, also demonstrate learning improvement in science. Parents rave about the quality of work (especially so early in the school year) that students produce to demonstrate their understanding of insects. They are happy to help plan, organize, and contribute the desserts and tea party. The best outcome of the nine-week celebration is the way students vocalize that our aim is being met. Students and parents ask me, "When do we get to do this again?" Finally, the second-grade students provide younger students (the supply) with great learning experiences while they watch the performance and visit our classroom museum.

The Seven Elements of a System

Supply for Our Classroom as a System

The supply is the future students who will be assigned to my classroom (Figure 1.2). Rather than dreading or worrying about some new students who

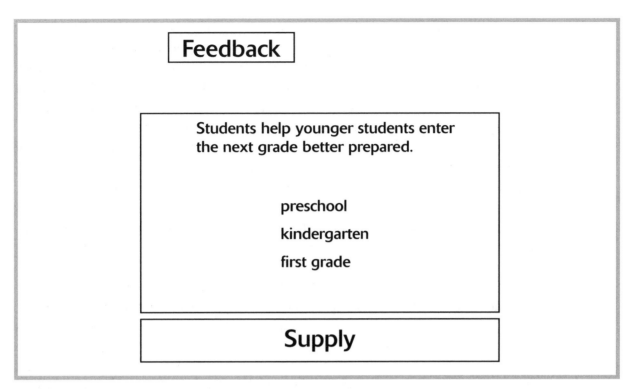

Figure 1.2. The supply for our classroom system.

arrive each fall from first grade, I've determined to influence the abilities of future second graders. Kindergarten teachers cannot improve their supply as easily, because they aren't as accessible as my future students. My future supply of second graders is right down the hall, in kindergarten and first grade.

Weekly, my class of twenty second graders works with our kindergarten pals to reinforce various skills involving computers, letter formation, spelling, writing, and reading. The kindergarten teacher and I assign the partners. As the year progresses, we continue to build flexible, working relationships to maintain enthusiasm while improving learning experiences. We read aloud the stories and books we publish in class to spread the joy of reading. The second-grade students take their jobs as "computer, writing, and reading teachers" very seriously.

At the end of one year, my kindergarten teaching partner attributed the fact that eleven of her twenty students began to read to our reading practice with them! It was thrilling to watch my students improve their fluency and expressive reading because they had such a receptive and appreciative audience of enthusiastic kindergartners. In less than an hour per week, the students built close friendships and helped each other in shared learning experiences.

Another example of helping our supply occurs when another first-grade teacher and I arrange to have our classes work together in shared reading experiences once a week. We read and discuss our favorite books from a wide range of genres. Each student seems to benefit from those enjoyable reading experiences. As with the kindergartners, my second-graders help younger students enter the next grade better prepared in language arts.

The majority of the first- and second-grade teachers at my school voluntarily participated and worked together in the California Reading and Literature Results Project, 1997–98. Various reading assessments were given each trimester to diagnose reading problems. The collected data are used to inform and improve our teaching practices to address individual student's reading needs.

Figures 1.3 through 1.10 are graphs created on Class Action™ software (whose use will be further explained later in this chapter) that demonstrate my classroom's performance for 1997–98 on each reading and spelling assessment. The following is a brief explanation of the assessments: The Yopp-Singer is a test of phoneme segmentation, while the Rosner tests auditory analysis (Figures 1.3 and 1.4). John Shefelbine's Basic Phonics Skills Test (BPST) assesses a student's phonic skills (Figure 1.5). Reading 200 HFW is an assessment of a student's ability to read the first two hundred high-frequency words from high-frequency word lists (Figure 1.6). The Bear Spelling Inventory helps determine where a student should be placed in his/her developmental spelling group, based on Dr. Donald Bear's research in *Words Their Way* (Figure 1.7). The K–3 Reading Results Project provides the first two hundred-word lists upon which my class's growth in spelling is assessed each trimester (Figure 1.8). The accuracy percentage class run chart demonstrates my class's performance at reading a specified grade-level text at 90 percent accuracy or better (Figure 1.9). Lastly, the state fluency class run chart displays my class's performance in reading fluency with a grade-level text (Figure 1.10). The results speak for themselves. Students improve because I adjust my teaching strategies and instruction, based upon the data I gather throughout the year.

The other teachers marveled at the data they gathered, and how the data helped them to improve the processes of teaching reading and spelling. Their efforts in the Results Project helped streamline the first and second grade's reading focus like nothing else in the five years of the school's existence. The data demonstrated we had "fewer failures and more successes."[8] We confidently claimed we did a better job of teaching reading that year—not only because the data proved it, but also because we observed an increased number of children who liked to read.

The primary teachers' volunteer participation in the CRLP Results Project is yet another example of teachers working together to improve the next grade level's supply. Each child's reading assessments, graphed data, and teacher's anecdotal records of effective teaching strategies are given to the new

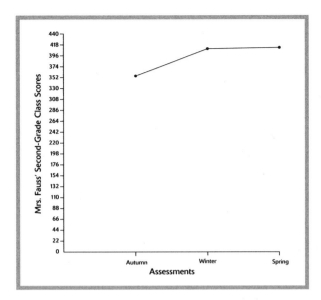

Figure 1.3. Yopp-Singer class run chart.

Figure 1.4. Rosner class run chart.

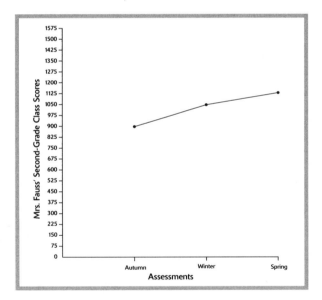

Figure 1.5. BPST Shefelbine class run chart.

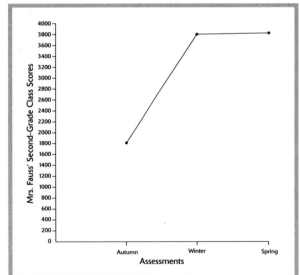

Figure 1.6. Reading 200 HFW class run chart.

teacher each year. In addition, same-grade teachers meet frequently to use process data to inform instruction.

The CRLP Results Project has finalized plans for another year of gathering and using data to improve instructional practices in reading, listening skills, and spelling. All the teachers who participated in 1997–98 are participating again during 1998–99. Also, more third-grade teachers will join our efforts at our school site. We plan to compare each year's data to the last, to

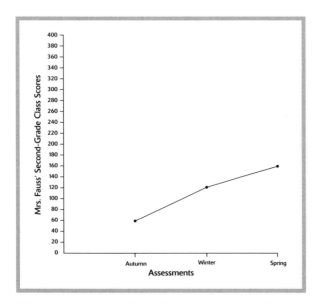

Figure 1.7. Bear Spelling Inventory class run chart.

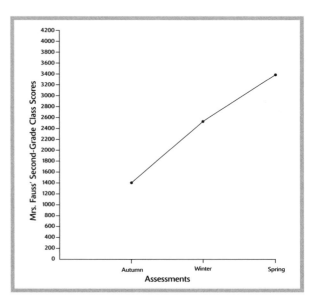

Figure 1.8. High-frequency spelling words class run chart.

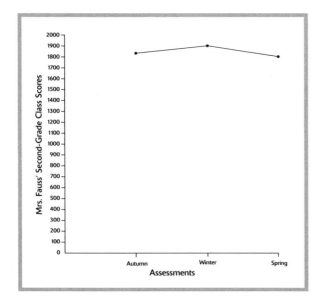

Figure 1.9. Accuracy percentage class run chart.

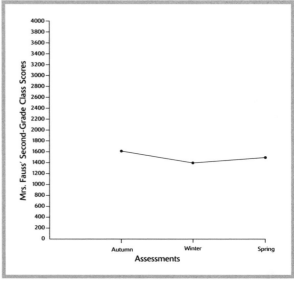

Figure 1.10. State fluency class run chart.

see if we have improved the system of teaching reading, listening skills, and spelling at our school.

A common sense of purpose united our efforts toward the goal of helping every child become a reader by the end of third grade. The success of the CRLP Results Project 1997–98 has had a ripple effect throughout our school, as we worked toward a common goal. It can be summed up in this way: "The three building blocks for improving schools are (1) a commitment to stop blaming; (2) the establishment of clear aims; and (3) agreement on a definition of improvement."[9]

Input into Our Classroom as a System

Input into our classroom system consists of the following ingredients: state standards, state standardized tests, the CRLP Results Project, district standards, Program Quality Review, expectations of parents, desires of students, special education programs, and student transiency. Each input has negative and positive connotations that impact our class as a system (Figure 1.11). Regarding input, Dr. Lee Jenkins states, "Most is from state and federal government. Input is not mentioned on traditional organizational charts. Legislators need to view education as a system for which they are responsible. Educators are not in control of the education system; it is controlled by non-educators elected to the legislatures or placed in judicial chairs."[10] Currently, "too many people in the public and in the media have the idea that being pro-education means pouring more billions of dollars down a bottomless pit to support the existing educational establishment. They will continue to believe that as long as no one says anything to the contrary,"[11] said Thomas Sowell, a nationally syndicated writer. Although a teacher must adhere to the input, he or she is still in control of the classroom system. The teacher must take the initiative to change it through continuous improvement processes. It becomes a grassroots attempt to change the educational system for the better.

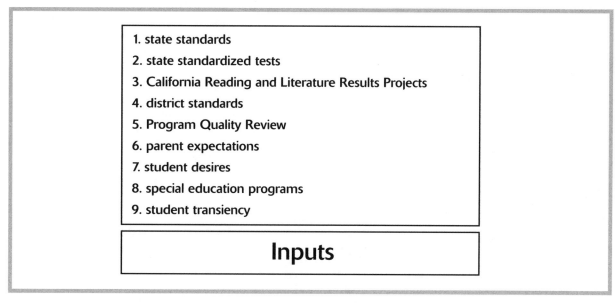

1. state standards
2. state standardized tests
3. California Reading and Literature Results Projects
4. district standards
5. Program Quality Review
6. parent expectations
7. student desires
8. special education programs
9. student transiency

Inputs

Figure 1.11. Inputs into our classroom system.

The Process of Our Classroom as a System

Robert Cornesky and William Lazarus state that "Quality must be built into every process before high-quality results can follow. Quality classrooms focus more on process improvement while setting high-quality expectations. Results do follow."[12] The process used in our classroom system (Figure 1.12) goes through continuous improvement within an organized collection of curricular units such as insects, amphibians (life science), family heritage and traditions (social science), solids and liquids (physical science), nutrition (health), air and weather (earth science), recycling, community, and geography. Every attempt has been made to ensure the units of study are developmentally appropriate for primary-age children. These units of study consistently capture the interest of the students each year. The students and I work together as a team to refine and improve the incremental steps in the process where concepts are learned and applied. Teaming with other grade levels (both higher and lower) also reinforces and enhances their experiences. We work through continuous improvement with a focus on the school district's aim, adapted from Deming's aim for education: "Maintain enthusiasm while increasing learning."[13]

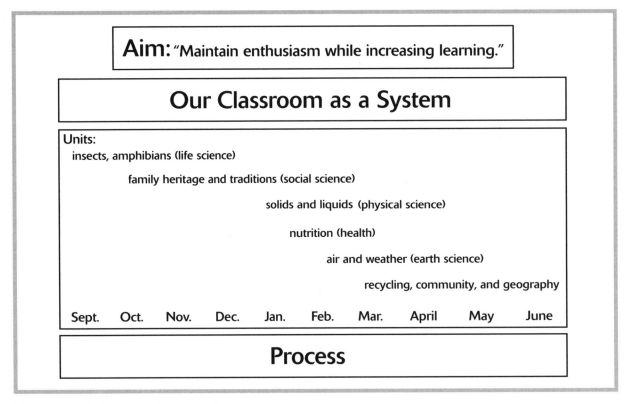

Figure 1.12. Process for our classroom system.

Output from Our Classroom as a System

The output from our classroom system (Figure 1.13) basically consists of results of the year-long learning process. The following are some examples:

1. Information: spelling and language pronunciation
   math concepts
   geography locations
   science facts
   art techniques
   history and chronology

2. Knowledge: writing and reading with understanding
   math problem-solving
   relating economy to geography
   using scientific methods
   producing artwork
   relating current events to the past[14]

3. Enthusiasm: monthly monitoring the joy of learning

4. Behavior: daily monitoring student behavior

Output is measured through various types of assessments. A few examples of formal assessments will be briefly explained in this chapter. Other successful teaching strategies, exercises, and assessments will be explained in subsequent chapters.

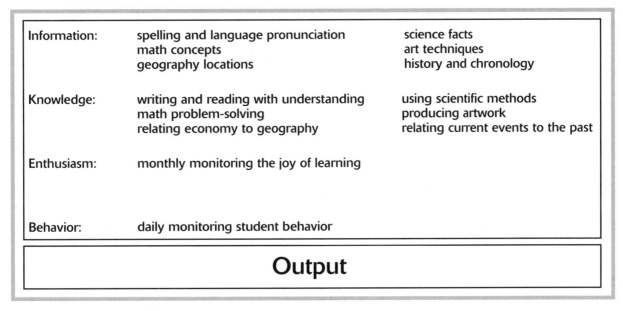

Information:	spelling and language pronunciation math concepts geography locations	science facts art techniques history and chronology
Knowledge:	writing and reading with understanding math problem-solving relating economy to geography	using scientific methods producing artwork relating current events to the past
Enthusiasm:	monthly monitoring the joy of learning	
Behavior:	daily monitoring student behavior	

Output

Figure 1.13. Output from our classroom system.

Spelling Assessments

One way spelling is assessed is by a weekly random preview/review test of high-frequency words. The process data are gathered, graphed, and studied to inform instruction. The commonly misspelled words are then practiced in sign language and with various other exercises. These are discussed thoroughly in chapter 4, with additional examples in Appendix A.

Writing Assessments

Writing is formally assessed using the district grade-level 6-point rubric. It is often informally assessed when students write with their third-grade and kindergarten buddies during weekly writing experiences.

Reading Assessments

Reading assessments include the assessment tools adopted by the California Reading and Literature Project/K–3 Reading Results. A brief overview of the assessments and graphs were explained earlier in this chapter.

Accelerated Readers™

A student signs up to take the comprehension test questions designed for each book. Students use the Macintosh™ version of Accelerated Reader™ as they complete a book. Each student's instructional reading level is determined by his responses to the timed assessment administered through the accompanying Star™ program. Each student is tested on the Star™ assessments at the beginning and end of each school year, in order to measure his growth in reading fluency and comprehension. The Star™ program calculates and issues diagnostic and growth reports for each student. The assessment results are studied and discussed with parents and students at conferences. As a team we share ways to help each child to improve his or her reading ability.

Monitoring monthly reading fluency

This is based on research from the University of Oregon[15] in recording student reading fluency. An end-of-the-year passage is selected, which is usually very challenging for students at the beginning of the year. Each month the student reads aloud the beginning of the same passage for one minute.

After the one-minute reading fluency check, the assessment can be extended to test comprehension by asking the student to retell the story. The teacher generates comprehension questions. This way, two forms of assessment, reading speed (fluency) and comprehension, can be taken from the same passage. A student's reading fluency increases as she makes gradual continuous improvement. The process data are used to make informed decisions to help the student improve his or her reading fluency. The data are graphed and shared with parents at conferences. Chapter 6 includes more information about successful reading strategies, goals, and expectations.

Math Assessments

Enterprise Weekly math concepts have been developed for kindergarten through eighth grade. Five mathematical concepts for second grade are assessed each Monday in my primary classroom: one review concept from kindergarten, two review concepts from first grade, and two preview concepts to be learned in second grade. It is a review/preview assessment developed from state standards. Concepts are selected randomly. The data gathered from the Enterprise Weekly are used to inform teacher instruction on subsequent days. Each Enterprise Weekly is organized in a math journal, where students are given additional individualized written lessons to extend or learn math concepts that are confusing or not yet understood. Many examples are given in chapter 5.

Science Assessments

The most important science facts to be learned during the current science unit are researched and compiled from the teacher resource binders. These facts are previewed/reviewed weekly through randomly selected science concepts. The process data are gathered, graphed, and used to inform instruction, in a way similar to the Enterprise Weekly.

Class Action™ Software

Student process data are graphed on Class Action™ software developed for educators. (See Appendix B for more information.) The data can be displayed as a whole-class scatter diagram with upper and lower limits of a control chart, class run chart, histogram, student run chart, or student run chart overlaid onto a class scatter diagram with upper and lower limits of a control chart. The graphs are used to display our class's weekly progress in math, spelling of high-frequency words, science facts, and reading fluency. Individual student graphs are printed frequently and shared with the family to update student progress. For every formal reporting period, graphs are attached to each student's report card.

The graphs are important means of communication. Students frequently have the opportunity to explain the whole-class progress graphs displayed in our classroom to visitors. Recently, one of my students was asked by an adult visitor what the graphs meant. She said, "They mean we are getting better in spelling, math, and science!" There will be many examples of these graphs and explanations throughout the following chapters.

Enthusiasm and Behavior Assessments

Enthusiasm and behavior are assessed by using quality tools such as issue bins and Plus Delta charts. Examples of how to use these tools are in the following chapters. Students self-evaluate their behavior daily. Examples are provided in the next section.

Customers

Our classroom system gathers feedback from the customers (Figure 1.14). The customers are my students, their parents, the next grade-level staff, and former students.

Feedback

Student Feedback

Each student monitors his or her own behavior daily on the self-evaluation forms[16] (Figure 1.15).

Each trimester when I issue a report card and graphs for each student, I ask my students to give me a report card in return (Figure 1.16).

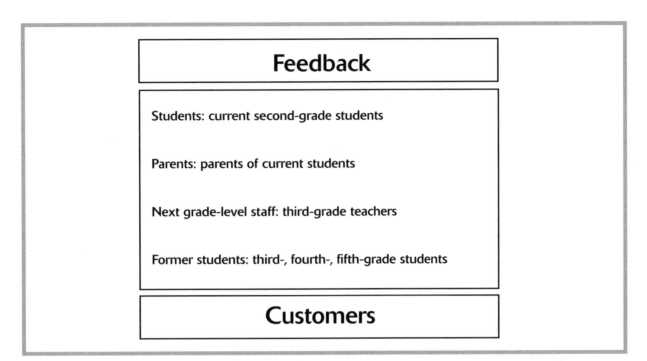

Figure 1.14. Customers and feedback in our classroom system.

Parent Feedback

Feedback is gathered about homework and student progress through a parent survey. The feedback helps me to keep the focus on continuously improving my classroom system (Figure 1.17).

Next Grade-Level Staff Feedback

Third-grade teachers are my customers. My students work weekly with their third-grade writing coaches in a third-grade classroom. The third-grade teacher and I evaluate and plan the writing lesson for the following week.

One very successful writing experience occurred when the second-graders interviewed the third-grade students. Then they switched roles. The questions were formed in a brainstorming session earlier in our own classrooms. From the answers given in the interview, the students wrote biographies of their writing partners. They then worked through the revision process, typed them on the computer, illustrated their self-portraits and acrostic poems (Figure 1.18), and placed the completed projects on our joint bulletin board in the main hallway. Our goal was to complete at least one project each month.

Student self-evaluation

Name:		Week of:			
Respect for Self and Others	Mon	Tues	Wed	Thurs	Fri
I listen while someone else is speaking.					
I come quietly into the room.					
I wait my turn to speak.					
I cooperate and contribute to my team's work.					
I use self-control and good manners.					
I respond promptly to directions.					
I help others when they ask me to.					
I do not disturb others with my voice or actions.					
Work and Study Habits					
I am ready to begin work.					
I do my best work and am proud of my work.					
I finish my work on time.					
Quality Improvement					
I made at least one suggestion to improve our class this week.			YES	NO	
I improved my work this week.			YES	NO	

Figure 1.15. Student self-evaluation.

TEACHER: _____ **GRADE:** _____
STUDENT: _____

GRADES: O = Outstanding   S = Satisfactory   N = Needs to improve

SUBJECT: Reading ☐

Describe the ways I have helped you to improve your reading._____
_____

How can reading activities be improved?_____
_____

SUBJECT: Writing and Spelling ☐

List your favorite writing and spelling activities:_____
_____

How can the writing and spelling activities be improved?_____
_____

SUBJECT: Math ☐

What are your favorite math activities?_____
_____

How can the math activities be improved?_____
_____

SUBJECT: Science ☐

What did you like about studying science?_____
_____

How can the science activities be improved?_____
_____

SUBJECT: Homework ☐

What are your favorite parts of the homework?_____
_____

What suggestions do you want to make to improve the homework?_____
_____

Are you working well with your table partner? yes ☐ no ☐ Why or why not? _____
_____

What other suggestions do you have to improve our classroom system?_____
_____

Figure 1.16. Teacher report card.

Dear Parents,

      Please circle the number that best represents your thoughts on the homework packets this trimester.

                     5 = Strongly agree
                     4 = Agree
                     3 = Neutral
                     2 = Somewhat disagree
                     1 = Disagree
               N/A = Not applicable

****

1.   My child had enough challenging homework each week.

      5   4   3   2   1

2.   Which parts of the homework were the most helpful to your child?

Reading daily in the library book.............................5 4 3 2 1 N/A

Reading daily in the phonics storybooks..............5 4 3 2 1 N/A

Reading daily in the Accelerated Reader™.........5 4 3 2 1 N/A

Spelling sentences/poems, phonogram practice...............5 4 3 2 1 N/A

Writing short reports or stories.............................5 4 3 2 1 N/A

Math problem-solving challenges...........................5 4 3 2 1 N/A

Optional math, science, social studies, and art projects...5 4 3 2 1 N/A

Please write any other helpful suggestions for improvement on the back. Your suggestions for improvement are greatly appreciated.

Thanks for taking the time to fill out this survey!

Sincerely,

Figure 1.17. Forms for parental feedback.

Dear Parents,
    Please take some time to give me some feedback about our year together.
I appreciate it!

1.   My child's most rewarding experiences this year were . . .

_____
_____
_____
_____
_____
_____
_____
_____

2.   I have noticed that my child has made excellent progress this year in . . .

_____
_____
_____
_____
_____
_____

3.   Helpful suggestions to improve the classroom system . . .

_____
_____
_____

Parent Signature_____ Phone #_____

Thanks for all your support. Together we have helped your child to succeed this
year. It has been an honor to work with you!

Sincerely,

Figure 1.17. Continued.

Figure 1.18. Student self-portrait and acrostic poem. Artwork by Patrick Howser. Used with permission.

I often speak with the third-grade teachers to check on former students. It is always interesting to see how the students are meeting their expectations in the third-grade curriculum. The teachers offer constructive feedback, helping me to better prepare the supply for the third-grade classroom by improving my second-grade classroom system.

Feedback from Former Students

"[A] very effective technique is to have older students buddy up to tutor younger students. . . . It makes the older student feel important and useful."[17] Such experiences allow older students to teach what they know, and to demonstrate a broad understanding of subjects as they work with my current students in reading and in math challenges. Positive leadership skills are practiced. Teaming younger and older students also seems to build a sense of community in our school. This is important, since a fourth-grade classroom is next to ours, and most of the nearby classrooms are third, fourth, and fifth grades.

An additional benefit of student tutoring is the opportunity to question former students and gather informal feedback on how to improve my primary classroom system. I learn from the brief interactions and observations as I watch my former students tutor the younger students.

The following examples are successful tutoring opportunities that the fourth- and fifth-grade teachers and I plan for our students.

The upper-grade teacher and I share a common goal: to provide a positive reading experience while improving our students' reading fluency. Once a week, fourth-grade students read with my second-grade students for about a half hour. To begin, we meet together for instructions and predetermine partner assignments in my classroom. After a brief discussion, the partners who wish to read silently take their books to the fourth-grade classroom. Those who wish to read aloud stay in my room and select second-grade-level texts to read together. This plan provides additional support for lower-level readers in both of our classrooms, while protecting their often fragile self-images. It seems safe to read aloud in second grade.

Throughout the day (when it doesn't interfere with the fourth-grade schedule) fourth-grade reading partners accompany two second-grade students to the library to choose a new Accelerated Reader™. These students have been taught by the librarian and classroom teachers how to use the computer to select and then locate a book from the second-grader's instructional reading level. It is also the fourth-grade student's responsibility to accompany the second-grade student back to class with the new book and the reading folder in a timely fashion.

One fifth-grade teacher sends some students from his class to my class twenty to thirty minutes daily as a reward for a job well done in his class. They help me teach individual students during our independent math time, which is approximately the last half hour of our morning schedule. These fifth-grade students are considered math experts. They and I circulate around the desks with pencil in hand, helping the second-grade students work through math problem-solving challenges. Each second-grade student must get our initials at the bottom of the math manipulative-based pages to signify she has proven her understanding of the concept. Then she is ready to tackle the problems on the next page. The older students revisit the math concepts they learned on a concrete level a few years prior and confirm many similar concepts that are taught at a more abstract level in fifth grade. The fifth-grade students work with my class until lunch. Before they return to their own classroom, they practice their leadership skills as they escort the younger students and me to the cafeteria.

Almost daily the other fifth-grade teacher sends two or three students over to my classroom to work one on one with my students as reading tutors. The second-grade students read through appropriately leveled books structured for success and enjoyment. Together they practice building fluency. The fifth-grade student usually clarifies and explains unknown vocabulary. Upon completion of the story, discussions about the story encourage student growth in reading comprehension. I gather valuable feedback from former students and current students as I observe them reading and working together. Their attitudes toward reading are very apparent. The feedback sends me on searches to locate properly leveled books written in their areas of interest. I rotate many books in and out of the book tubs while keeping their favorite books to be revisited again and again.

The valuable feedback I gather from former second-grade students, now fourth and fifth graders, and from my current second graders helps me evaluate my math and reading programs. These observations and student feedback lead to informed decisions to improve my classroom system. "Thus young students develop bonds with older students. This technique often

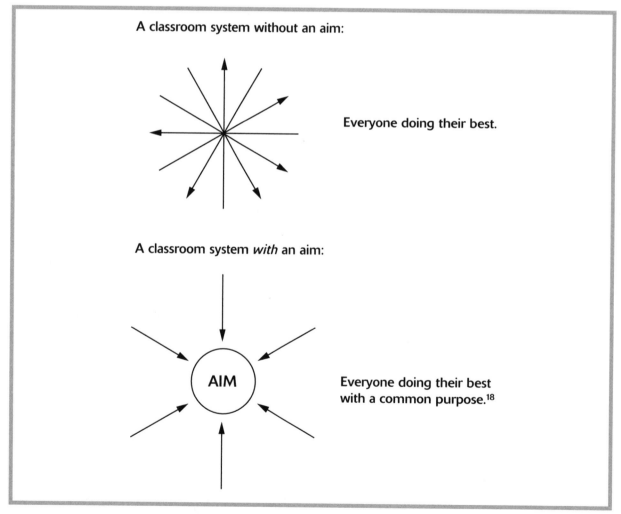

Figure 1.19. Aim of the classroom system.

makes everyone within the school feel that they share a common goal or purpose. This is truly a unifying force."[19] There's nothing new about fourth and fifth graders helping second graders. What is new, however, is my attitude of looking to former students for feedback regarding how to improve my classroom system.

In summary, six out of a system's seven elements are supply, inputs, process, outputs, customers, and feedback. The manager of any system has the responsibility to ensure that all the components work in synchrony, toward a common goal. Encompassing the whole system is the seventh element, the aim. It influences all the parts and provides a common sense of purpose and focus as a system continuously improves.

Aim

The aim is the most important part of a system (Figure 1.19). It is a concise statement of purpose for the classroom system. It will be described at length in the beginning of the next chapter.

Notes

1. Helio Gomes, *Quality Quotes* (Milwaukee, WI: ASQC, Quality Press, 1996), 138.
2. W. Edwards Deming, American Association of School Administrators, Washington, DC, January 1992.
3. Lee Jenkins, personal e-mail, 21 Nov. 1998.
4. Lee Jenkins, *Improving Student Learning* (Milwaukee, WI: ASQ Quality Press, 1997), 49.
5. Ibid., 48.
6. Ibid., 4.
7. Ibid.
8. Ibid., 5.
9. Ibid., 13.
10. Ibid., 21–22.
11. Thomas Sowell, "GOP Lost Because It Wouldn't Speak Out." *Record Searchlight* (Redding, CA), 7 Nov. 1998, Sec. A, p. 6.
12. Robert Cornesky and William Lazarus, *Continuous Quality Improvement in the Classroom: A Collaborative Approach* (Port Orange, FL: Cornesky & Associates, 1995), 22.
13. Lee Jenkins, *Improving Student Learning* (Milwaukee, WI: ASQ Quality Press, 1997), 115.
14. Ibid., 23–24.
15. Lee Jenkins, *Applying Quality Principles in Schools* (Cedar Rapids, IA: AASA Total Quality Network, 1995), 19.
15. Margaret Byrnes and Robert Cornesky, *Quality Fusion* (Port Orange, FL: Cornesky & Associates, 1994), 136.
17. Ibid., 114.
18. Lee Jenkins, *Improving Student Learning* (Milwaukee, WI: ASQ Quality Press, 1997), 164.
19. Byrnes and Cornesky, p. 114.

CHAPTER 2

Building a Community of Positive Relationships

> *"Mission starts with determining what you really care about and want to accomplish, and committing yourself to it. You can always develop expertise."*
>
> CHARLES GARFIELD[1]

T he aim is the fuel that drives the system. It is strategically placed in Figure 1.1 above "Our Classroom as a System," with arrows drawn to connect each component. This signifies that it feeds into each component of the system.

The Aim

Ralph Waldo Emerson once said, "Nothing great was ever achieved without enthusiasm. And true enthusiasm comes from giving ourselves to a purpose."[2] Since 1993, I have enthusiastically given myself to the purpose of teaching my second-grade students an integrated curriculum that focuses on the district's aim, which is adapted from Dr. Deming's aim for education: "Maintain enthusiasm while increasing learning."[3] On the district's website, the superintendent commented, "For too long schools have accepted the responsibility to motivate students to learn, when probably a better strategy is to understand that kindergartners enter the K–12 systems very motivated to learn, and the responsibility of educators is to figure out what's causing a loss of enthusiasm and change the practices. Even though we don't have the answers to loss of enthusiasm, the Enterprise staff has committed themselves to maintaining enthusiasm while increasing learning."[4]

Putting the Aim into Classroom Practice

I focus on the aim because I want my students to look forward to learning each day. The challenge for me as a teacher is to protect, support, and maintain their natural enthusiasm for learning. Nurturing relationships and providing meaningful instruction based on their interests, experiences, and developmental abilities is my obvious assignment as their second-grade teacher. Every week, I check the effectiveness of my teaching strategies by collecting and graphing data from student assessments. The data help me to gain insight into each new group of students. I have to adjust and find effective teaching practices to accommodate the needs of my students, while striving for continuous improvement in my classroom system. The process I just described is based on the PDSA cycle or the Deming cycle. It was originally developed by Dr. Walter Shewhart and modified by Dr. Deming. In honor of his mentor, Dr. Deming always referred to it as the Shewhart cycle (Figure 2.1).[5]

"The PDSA cycle is a simple, effective data-driven instrument for continuous learning and improvement."[6]

"The PDSA cycle has the following steps.

Plan

1. Determine current system production.

2. Analyze data for causes of poor production results.

3. Envision improvement.

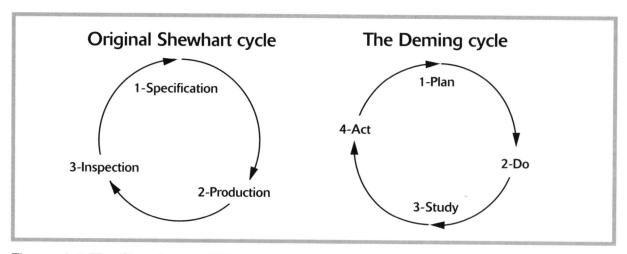

Figure 2.1. The Shewhart and Deming cycles.

Do

4. Decide which improvement theory to attempt.

5. Implement theory.

Study

6. Study results of experiment.

Act

7. Establish the changes which resulted in improvements, as organizational norms.

8. Start over."[7]

The students and I tenaciously work within that model to "maintain enthusiasm while increasing learning"[8] throughout the year.

District Mission Statement

The district's mission statement on our webpage states that our mission is to develop the full potential of each student's intellectual, ethical, physical, creative, cultural, social, and technological capabilities. This will be accomplished by providing meaningful instruction and building a community of positive relationships. We are dedicated to maximizing the expertise and human potential of every staff member because we recognize that an exemplary staff, working as partners with parents, is the key to student development.[9]

The District Mission Statement in Classroom Practice

Each new school year, with this mission statement in mind, I initiate communication with my new students and their parents to build "a community of positive relationships."[10] Establishing a positive relationship also encourages mutual trust, which begins to grow and flourish. I take my brand-new supply of first-graders (and their parents) and begin a relationship built on trust. It must be a priority "to persuade all your students to trust you. They must believe that, in all you ask them to do as well as in how you ask them to do it, you are on their side."[11] Consider two other practical reasons why building trust is so important: First, if I cannot trust my second graders in our classroom, how can I expect to trust them when they are out of the classroom working with their kindergarten buddies, or sharing completed projects with first- and second-grade friends, third-grade writing coaches, and fourth-grade reading partners? Second, if my new parents are uninformed or confused about my program, how can they affirm my efforts to build a team of support for their child's growth and development in our classroom system? In this chapter, I will offer examples and explanations of how the students and I use many quality principles at the beginning of the year. Upon this foundation I work on the premise of "providing meaningful instruction"[12] from state frameworks, district standards, and adopted curriculum guidelines, with the goal of continuously improving all facets of my classroom system.

Teacher-Initiated Communication

Three weeks before the school year begins, I send a short letter to each student, inviting him or her into the classroom for a sneak preview. Next, I write a more detailed letter to each family to welcome them to our classroom. (These examples are an early attempt to establish trust.) These letters are not only designed to welcome them, but also to build anticipation about what will happen in a few short weeks. Many children are becoming bored with summer vacation at this point and welcome news about the forthcoming year. In the letter to the parents I portray myself as a team player in support of their child. I make it clear that I expect their child to succeed in our classroom. This teacher-initiated communication produces positive responses from the students and their families. The following letters are examples of positive teacher-initiated communication that attempts to build a trusting relationship with each family before school starts.The letter shown in Figure 2.2 is sent to my new students.

Figure 2.3 shows a letter I send to the entire family. It welcomes them and extends an invitation to visit Room 17 during the "sneak preview" of the classroom. It also gives a brief overview of our schedule and classroom policies and procedures.

"Sneak Preview" of the Classroom

Opening up the classroom a few days before school begins is another way to build relationships based on trust. The students get a "sneak preview" of the classroom. Since many students are afraid of what they don't know, this experience helps drive out some fear the students may have of starting a new year. It helps to make the transition from first grade to second grade go more smoothly. Students and their families become acquainted with the location of their new classroom. At our school site, the first- and second-grade classrooms are located at opposite ends of the buildings. Moving to second grade provides them with important new challenges, like finding new bathroom locations and the way to the playground for recess.

It is imperative that the new students sense that I value their uniqueness and give the gift of acceptance to each one. My job as their teacher is to determine each's preferred learning styles and create opportunities for them to feel successful. I have to communicate high, but reasonable and attainable, academic and social expectations for each of them. My job as their second-grade teacher is to prepare them for third grade and beyond. Having the classroom organized and ready for their preview visit a few days before school begins demonstrates my expectation that they will begin to work on the first day of school.

Roses are red
Violets are blue
On August 21st
I get to see you!
You are invited to attend Room 17's "sneak preview," from 11:00–12:00 in Mrs. Fauss' Class!

Figure 2.2. Note to new students.

Dear Families,

Welcome to our classroom family. I anticipate a very exciting and productive year as we work toward continuous improvement!

Please read through our typical weekly schedule and brief explanations of classroom policies and procedures.

Monday–Thursday Schedule

7:50 A.M.	Primary recess
8:00 A.M.	**Class begins***
8:00–9:00	Class job chart, class pledge, flag salute, singing/music, poetry, and pocket chart work. Spelling sentences with explicit phonics instruction, integrated science/social science themes, and math problem-solving challenges.
9:00–9:30	Reading teams
9:30–9:50	Primary recess
9:50–10:40	Children's literature/poetry read-aloud. Integrated art, science, and district core literature.
10:45–11:10	Independent study in math concepts
11:15–12:00	Lunch
12:00–12:20	P.E.
12:20–12:30	Student of the Week sharing time
12:30–12:55	Literacy centers: Reading and language arts skills and word study/spelling practice. Self-selected reading/Accelerated Reading Program.
12:55–1:25	Writing Folders (Wednesdays: third-grade writing coaches) (Thursdays: fourth-grade reading partners)
1:25–1:30	Self-evaluation, Plus Delta chart
1:30	Read-aloud novel
1:45	Class dismissal

*A child must be marked tardy if he/she arrives after this time. If he/she arrives after 7:50 A.M., check him/her in with the office personnel. They will issue a class admittance slip.

Friday Schedule

7:40–7:50	Primary recess
7:50	Class begins
8:00–8:30	Library
8:30–8:55	Music
9:00–9:25	Spelling
9:25–9:45	Primary recess
9:45–10:40	Children's literature/poetry read-aloud. Reading teams and language arts skills and spelling practice.
10:45–11:10	Independent study of math concepts

Figure 2.3. Letter to new parents: Overview of daily schedules.

11:15–12:00   Lunch
12:05–12:30   Computer lab or writing lesson or reading with kindergarten buddies
12:30–1:00   Literacy centers: Writing projects, phonics/phonogram books
1:00–1:30   Art
1:30–1:35   Self-evaluations
1:35–1:45   Read-aloud novel
1:45   Class dismissal

Parent Volunteers

You will have an opportunity to sign up during our first meeting in Room 17 on Thursday from 11:00–12:00. We will all benefit from your time and help! Thanks so very much for considering becoming a volunteer in our classroom. You can be part of a team that will help children be successful in their learning experiences!

Discipline

Good behavior is consistently recognized and rewarded in our classroom. The children are daily working as a whole group to earn a "great behavior celebration." I use a color chart to provide a visual reminder of how each child is handling self-management during the day. I send home a small report on your child's completed work packets in the homework envelope each Friday. Please note the following explanation of each color and what it represents.

Green: Self-manager
Yellow: Warning and an opportunity to try again
Orange: Loss of privilege
Red: Child makes phone call to parents
Navy Blue: Severe problem, reported to the principal

Occasionally, I may need to stay in at recess with your child to help him/her with incomplete work or clear up problems with math and reading concepts. Additionally, I may need to hold a student in if he/she needs some extra help in monitoring his/her behavior and understanding how to get along with others. This classroom and the playground need to be safe and happy learning environments, and I will do everything in my power to help each of my students make it exactly that!

In conclusion, hopefully, this lengthy letter has informed and answered possible questions and concerns you may have had. My goal this year is to communicate often with you about your wonderful son or daughter. I will be willing to discuss and work with you toward designing a solution to any problem that may arise. I am looking forward to teaming with you this year on behalf of your child! Working together as a team will help your child succeed.

I'm looking forward to visiting you at the "sneak preview" of our classroom, Room 17, 11:00–12:00. Our Booster Club is sponsoring a whole-school BBQ from 12:00–2:00 P.M. Please come and join the welcome-back celebration!

Figure 2.3. Continued.

> A quality leader maintains high expectations and uses whatever empowerment methods are necessary to gain student and parent commitment to achieving them. In addition, the quality leader recognizes that having high expectations is not enough; one must know how and with what means one can demonstrate and help students achieve them.[13]

Working through the continuous improvement processes, we, as a team of learners, will be expected to contribute and produce quality work. The classroom setting and my demeanor must consistently demonstrate this expectation.

As the families arrive to participate in the sneak preview, they are greeted by signs on both classroom entryway doors that say, "I am so glad you are here!" Once inside the classroom they see a large banner high on the classroom wall that states "You will all Succeed!"[14] (It is a scaled-down interpretive sample of Enterprise School District's mission statement.) A musical selection from the Baroque period plays quietly in the background for their listening enjoyment. It has a soothing and calming effect on the children. I am able to greet each child and family personally, in a relaxed and friendly atmosphere.

First impressions become lasting expectations. Students and their families find many enticing science artifacts on the counter, which invite the children to touch and explore. We are going to learn about science daily. A banner near the ceiling says "We are Scientists." The classroom is full of books organized in tubs near the front open carpet area and on each available shelf. A banner above the main classroom library says, "We are Readers," framed with sleeves of several favorite children's books. We are going to read a lot, every day. Other banners say "We are Writers" and "We are Artists" above their personal bulletin boards. Again the expectation is subtly implied: we will be writing and illustrating many stories. The "We are Musicians" banner is above the piano. We will be singing and illustrating our own songbooks, to share with our kindergarten pals and our families every other week. At the end of the year, each child will take home a collection of songs we share together. Charts of poetry are sprinkled around the room in pocket charts and on cupboard doors. Also, a poem (with high-frequency words highlighted) is attached to the back of each student's chair. We will be chanting, memorizing, and performing poetry. A collection of favorite poems will be sent home at the end of the year. All of the banners and poems help to present, in a visual way, my belief system about the abilities of each child:

Students tend to learn as little or as much as their teachers expect. Teachers who set and communicate high expectations to all their students obtain greater academic performance from these students than teachers who set low expectations.[15]

The rest of the wall space is basically blank except for the first and second high-frequency-words posters. Motivational posters and signs do not seem to make much impact on the children. Students attend to and celebrate what they themselves produce. The walls will soon be decorated with student work. It has been my experience that children quickly take ownership of a classroom as they see their writing assignments and artwork displayed on the personal bulletin boards around the room. Each personal bulletin board is made simply by stapling two 12″ × 18″ pieces of construction paper, one above the other, onto the wall. During the first week of school, students decorate their names and draw self-portraits on 12″ × 18″ pieces of white construction paper, cut into fourths: one-fourth of a sheet is given to each student. After each child prints his name in large letters with a black marker, he decorates it with other colored markers. These are placed above the two larger pieces of paper, which become the background for the personal bulletin board.

I have observed that the parents and children need a sense of where their established place or self-space is located in the new classroom. Through student input and teacher observation, we will be working with several flexible grouping possibilities. As a class, we will be discussing ways to arrange the desks to accomplish the most work. The students will discover that their best friend may not be the person with whom they work best.

As the parents, students, and I visit with each other, a new classroom family of learners is being established. This positive personal interaction with families helps to set the tone for the year. It is amazing how much trust and respect begins to develop in just an hour or so. I remind the parents that I want to work as a partner with each of them, helping their child succeed in our classroom. This is reinforced by asking parents to volunteer in the classroom and to fill out take-home surveys about their children.

I ask them to communicate in writing because in the past some parents have cornered me and insisted on telling their child's life history in front of a roomful of other parents and children, often embarrassing their own child. My time was sometimes monopolized by a few aggressive but well-meaning parents who hindered me from greeting and interacting with *all* of my new families. Giving the parents the take-home survey encourages them to put thought and effort into sharing the strengths, perceived needs, and goals they have for their children in the privacy of their own homes. The written survey conveys the fact that I consider them experts on their children and value their opinions. The completed survey and information sheets are placed in each child's portfolio as a reference for the year. I often refer to the surveys to assess the children's progress toward stated goals.

Figure 2.4 shows a new-parent communication letter that explains my classroom's features and philosophies. Figure 2.5 shows a student information form given to the new parents before school begins.

After a short presentation I invite them to again circulate and investigate our classroom. I am available for questions and conversation. As the parents and students leave the classroom, many adults comment that they wish they could have had such a positive beginning experience when they were in grade school.

Other primary teachers who start the new year this way and I shared the positive aspects of this adventure with other staff members. As we discussed it with our colleagues, we hoped this positive way of beginning the new year would be adopted by the rest of the staff. We believed it would benefit the whole school climate, since we had each experienced so many benefits in our own classrooms. We wanted to improve our system for beginning the school year. It was an early attempt to attend to some of the student's five basic needs, as outlined by Dr. William Glasser in *The Quality School Teacher*[16]: survival, love/respect, power, fun, and freedom.

Fortunately, this became a reality the following year, due to our efforts and the help of our very supportive administrator. During a staff meeting in late spring, our principal challenged us to open our classrooms for an hour, followed by a whole-school barbecue sponsored by our parent booster club and a local fast-food restaurant. The rest of the staff enthusiastically embraced the idea, and it became a reality the following August.

The Thursday before school officially opened, every teacher had his classroom ready and open for new students and parents to visit. We found it to be a very fun and exciting way to celebrate the beginning of another school year. This event helped to bond the staff and students as we anticipated another great year together. Many of the families' fears of the unknown seemed to dissipate. It was so well received by teachers and families that plans were made to schedule it as an annual event.

The students and I start our first official day of school much more smoothly because we have already experienced many of the typical "first-day jitters" the previous Thursday. Students and parents arrive the first day of school with positive exchanges and smiles on their faces, illustrating "a basic belief of the psychology category of profound knowledge . . . that everyone comes [to school] wanting to do a good job."[17] The responsibility

Dear Family,

I am excited to be your child's teacher this year! We'll continue to learn about each other and our world as we focus on becoming better readers, writers, artists, mathematicians, scientists, and citizens. Below are some of the features and philosophies that I have in my classroom. I hope this information will strengthen your connection to your child's classroom. I hope this will also strengthen your connection to your child's education and give you a feel for what your child will experience each day in Room 17.

Language Arts

Reading

An important part of my program (based on my experiences during continuous training in reading and spelling research at the California Reading and Literature Results Projects) is that you listen and interact with him/her at home each night while your child practices the reading strategies and phonics skills we work on during class. **(The Bookmark page in the homework packet has some helpful suggestions.)** If you need more suggestions, I will do my best to help you use your special abilities as a parent to help your child improve his/her reading skills in the home reader. (Please keep me posted through notes, phone calls, or just come on in to communicate how your child is reading in the home reader.) When the reader is completed, please send it back to class so I may check your child's progress. If the reader is not working as your child and I anticipated, send it back and I will reevaluate the home reader and send a different one. It is time-consuming, often hard work, but very worthwhile. Reading opens the door of understanding to all other curriculums. You and I are a team helping your child enjoy success with reading!

Spelling

I'll challenge your child with developmentally appropriate letter and word puzzles to help him/her see word families and common spelling patterns. Your child will be taught the first two hundred high-frequency words in the English language (developed by a spelling researcher) through poetry, sentences, and songs. (These are the underlined or **bold** words in the spelling sentences your child has been practicing daily.) The attached lists of words are the main words your child will be responsible to learn this whole year. We will be learning and reviewing them over and over in different contexts. Your child graphs his/her progress each week. I'll print out a copy of your child's progress for you to keep at conference time. The last four years I have had great success with my spelling program. I will do my best to make it fun and interesting for your child!

In addition to spelling practice, your child will have many opportunities to learn how to read the rest of the one thousand high-frequency words. (If you would like to practice more than the first two hundred words with your child, please request a copy of the rest of the one thousand words.) When your child demonstrates consistent, correct spelling of the first two hundred words, I will give him/her the next level to keep challenging your child. I try very hard to individualize a student's

Figure 2.4. New-parent communication letter: Classroom features and philosophies.

learning whenever possible. We will sing, speak, recite poetry, move, and perform. We plan and work closely together. We are anticipating that the rest of the year will be full of excitement and fun learning experiences.

Writing

Daily we will be writing in our own class about real life experiences in all the curricular areas, as well as responses to core literature. Your child will be teamed up with a third-grade writing coach. We will be working together weekly on writing processes. In order to teach what we know about writing, we will be helping our kindergarten pals with their writing experiences each week. They will get to enjoy and celebrate with us all of the illustrated books and stories we publish in our classroom.

Social Studies

During November and December we will celebrate our families and our traditions, learn quilting and about other cultures' traditions, and have several unique art experiences. During the end of April and most of May, we will be learning about recycling, our community of Redding, and mapping skills. Throughout the whole year we will be working together to build a positive community of learners in our classroom. Each student will have the opportunity to be Student of the Week. During that week your child will have daily opportunities to share about himself and his family. A book of stories written by each student will be compiled especially for the Student of the Week.

Math

In math we will be reviewing and extending the concepts they have worked with in kindergarten and first grade, such as addition/subtraction facts 0–20, measuring, regrouping, borrowing, multiplication, division, time (to the minute), money (making change to a dollar), fractions, place value, probability, statistics, geometry, algebraic equations, and manipulation of large numbers. Most importantly, we will work on thinking and explaining mathematically. We will describe how we get answers, draw pictures to go with story problems, and talk about faster (more efficient) ways to figure out an answer. To do this we will be using many manipulatives, as well as the traditional paper and pencil tasks that have been used for generations to cement concepts and provide added practice.

Science

My science program was developed by scientists at Lawrence Hall of Science at UC Berkeley. It is developmentally appropriate for second grade. We will do a lot of learning by doing, observing, and communicating, as well as more traditional methods of reading and talking to experts (scientific research). Most importantly, our young scientists will have the opportunity to become better mathematicians as we gather and quantify data, and better writers, readers, and spellers as we learn and report on what we know. The science themes this year will include insects, amphibians, solids and liquids, nutrition, air and weather, and recycling.

Figure 2.4. Continued.

Physical Education

Students will be learning P.E. skills and motor development in a program by Cliff Carnes and another by Robin Cook.

Thank you for taking time out of your busy schedule to read this information about our class schedule this year. If you have any questions or concerns, please feel welcome to call me at school or at home. Your constructive suggestions and advice are always appreciated!

Sincerely,

Figure 2.4. Continued.

Dear Parent(s),

Please help me get to know your child better by completing this information sheet and returning it to me by Friday, August 28th. It will be placed in your child's classroom file as a reference.

Child's full name: _____

Child prefers to be called (nickname): _____

1. My child's strengths are:

_____

_____

_____

2. My child needs most help in:

_____

_____

_____

3. My child best learns new skills by (seeing, hearing, doing):

_____

4. The most frustrating school experiences for my child have been:

_____

_____

_____

Figure 2.5. Student information form.

5. The most rewarding school experiences for my child have been:

_____

_____

_____

_____

6. The three major goals I have for my child, _____ , this year are:

   1. _____

   2. _____

   3. _____

7. My child is allergic to:

_____

8. Some things I would like you to know about my child are:

_____

_____

_____

_____

9. My child has special interests in:

_____

_____

_____

_____

Parent Signature _____ Phone # _____

Thanks for your help. This information will assist me in planning an educational experience that will best meet your child's needs. As partners we can help your child succeed!

Sincerely,

Figure 2.5. Continued.

of the teacher is to nurture that basic belief while providing meaningful learning experiences until the last day of school.

In summary, with the aim and mission statement in focus, the PDSA cycle is used to manage learning. The students and families will listen and work with the teacher when he or she proves to be trustworthy. Gradually, children will begin to take ownership in the classroom system as they believe their opinions and input are valued and implemented. Every possible effort should be made to use their suggestions and feedback to improve the classroom system.

Notes

1. Charles Garfield, *Peak Performers* (New York, NY: Avon, 1983), 96.
2. Margaret Byrnes and Robert Cornesky, *The Quality Teacher* (Bunnell, FL: Cornesky & Associates, 1992), 39.
3. Lee Jenkins, *Improving Student Learning*, (Milwaukee, WI: ASQ Quality Press, 1997), 115.
4. Enterprise School District's website: *Mission Aim* (Redding, CA: http://www.enterprise.k12.ca.us, 1998), district page.
5. John Jay Bonstingl, *Schools of Quality* (Alexandria, VA: ASCD, 1996), 9.
6. Ibid., 10.
7. Jenkins, *Improving Students Learning*, 130.
8. Ibid., 115.
9. Enterprise website (see note 4).
10. Ibid.
11. William Glasser, *The Quality School Teacher: A Companion Volume to "The Quality School"* (New York, NY; Harper Collins Publishers, 1993), 26.
12. Enterprise website (see note 4).
13. M. Byrnes and R. Cornesky, *Quality Fusion* (Port Orange, FL: Cornesky & Associates, 1995), 36.
14. Harry Wong, *The First Days of School* (Sunnyvale, CA: Harry K. Wong Publications, 1991), 48.
15. U.S. Department of Education, *What Works: Research about Teaching and Learning* (Washington DC: Government Printing Office, 1986), 7.
16. Glasser, *The Quality School Teacher,* 19.
17. Byrnes and Cornesky, *The Quality Teacher,* 33.

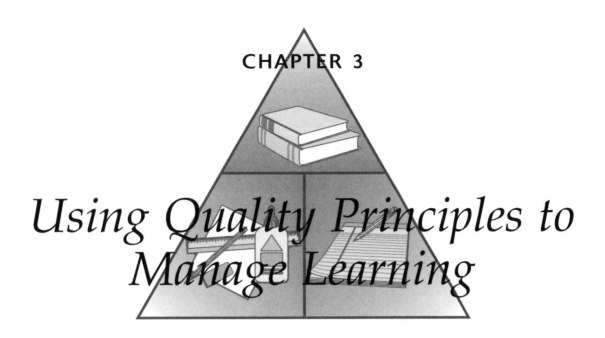

CHAPTER 3

Using Quality Principles to Manage Learning

"The classic tools of TQM are thinking tools. Where measurement is used, it is an aid to understanding and decision-making, not as an end in itself."

MURGATROYD AND MORGAN[1]

My class establishes our management system for learning during the first weeks of school, using many quality principles. These principles are based on the belief that "everyone comes [to school] wanting to do a good job."[2] It is a basic belief of the psychology section of Deming's profound knowledge. Faulty processes are what keep everyone from being successful.

Affinity Diagram

The students and I begin to establish a sense of purpose for being in second grade. I ask the students, "What do you want to learn in second grade?" (No discussion is allowed at this time.) The children write their ideas on Post-It™ notes. All written responses are accepted and posted on the board. Then we discuss and rearrange the ideas into natural groupings. The categories are labeled. After the ideas are discussed together, they are put into statements and written on a chart and displayed in the classroom. This process creates an affinity diagram.

Fishbone Diagram

Once we clarify why we are at school, the next issue is to address behavior expectations. After reading a story that addresses student behavior, we construct a negative fishbone to identify the negative characteristics of the misbehaved children in the story (Figure 3.1).

Next, we draw a positive fishbone to show what positive characteristics we want to have in our classroom (Figure 3.2). (I modeled the fishbone diagrams after Carol Quaranta's example lesson in *Tools in Action '98*, Leander ISD, Texas.)

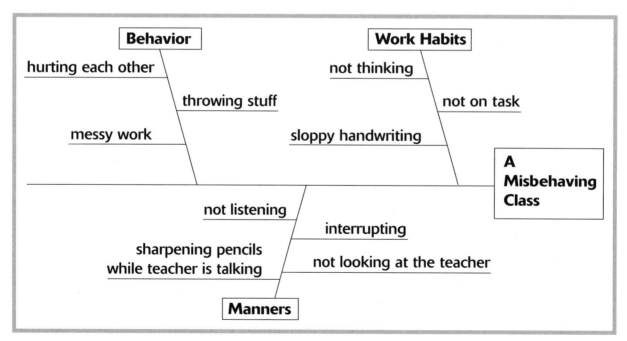

Figure 3.1. Negative fishbone diagram.

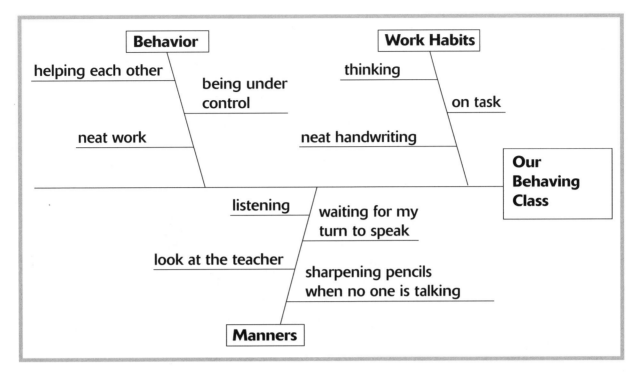

Figure 3.2. Positive fishbone diagram.

The fishbone diagrams help the students to focus on cause and effect. An effect from the story is written in the large rectangle—the fish head. We label the fishbones with many causes that influence the effect. The negative fishbone illustrates how we do not want to behave in our classroom. The positive fishbone provides an excellent way to begin generating the classroom rules for acceptable behavior in our classroom.

I set the stage for acceptance of all shared ideas to establish our classroom rules. Ideas are generated from the positive fishbone. Any rules that are not understood are discussed for clarification. Similar ideas are grouped together, and each category or group is labeled with a title. The rules are listed in positive statements on a piece of chart paper. Every student signs it. The list of rules will become the class pledge we read together aloud as we begin each morning.

The following is an example of a class pledge:

Today I will do my best.
I will be honest.
I will respect others.
I will care for all property.
I will be quiet in the hallway.
I will control my hands and feet.

I can learn.
I will learn.

(Our class pledge was inspired from the example Mrs. Chronicle made with her class at Central Elementary School in Linden, Michigan.)

Writing lessons can be easily developed from the class pledge chart. Ideas are generated by brainstorming. The goal is to stimulate children to write about the class pledge, one line at a time. All of the students' ideas are written onto the white board. The statement "Today I will do my best," is copied onto the top line in *My Book of Rules* (Figures 3.3 and 3.4). (Master skills booklet covers and inside sheet, designed by Dr. Lee Jenkins, are included in Appendix C. Used with permission.) An illustration is drawn in the circle, followed by an explanation of the rule on the lines provided at the bottom of the page. Since there are some extra pages in the booklet, students choose other important rules to add such as outside recess rules. Student volunteers share their work and act out a role play or pantomime of the rule. "If students use pantomime, they will engage in kinesthetic learning and develop brain hemispheres to understand" the rule.[3]

The students need to develop a sense of ownership of our classroom system. It is always worth the time to stop, clarify, and discuss the purpose of a rule we have previously made. As the year progresses, we often modify our original rules as students offer suggestions with the intent of improving our classroom system. Rules are added or deleted from the original class pledge list when the children and I decide it is necessary.

Force Field Analysis

Another quality tool, the force field analysis, is useful when comparing negative and positive behaviors in another lesson. It can be drawn on chart paper or on the board (Figure 3.5 and 3.6).

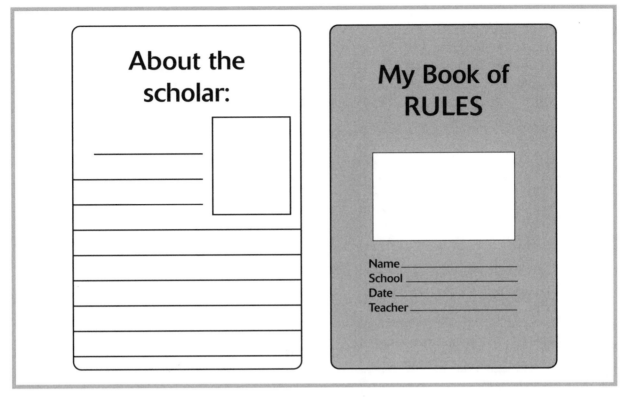

Figure 3.3. Front and back cover of *My Book of Rules.*

Students Empowered in Classroom Jobs

Teachers are those who use themselves as bridges, over which they invite their students to cross; then having facilitated their crossing, joyfully collapse, encouraging them to create bridges of their own.

Nikos Kazantzakis[4]

As the teacher, my role is to be a team leader who coaches, facilitates, collaborates, and monitors each student's academic and social growth. As the team leader, I must train future leaders. It is my responsibility to provide classroom jobs that purposely promote and nourish leadership qualities. After all, "the best leaders are those who believe in power and empowerment." "The most effective approach to leadership focuses on others—emphasizes the growing competence of everyone in the organization [classroom]." "When you

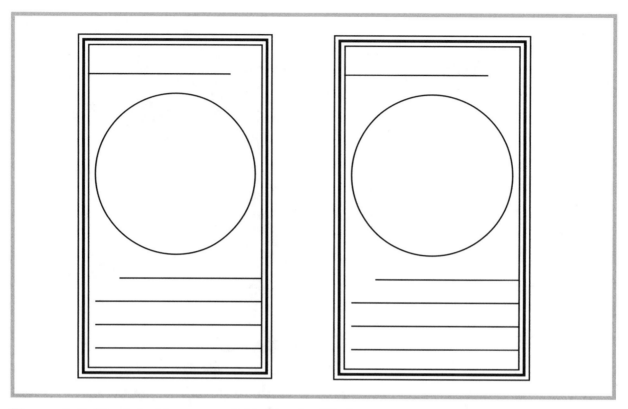

Figure 3.4. Blank inside pages of *My Book of Rules*.

make others feel significant and competent, you will yourself be regarded as significant and competent."[5]

Empowerment
is the art of increasing
the competence and capability of others
by endowing them with a sense of self-worth and potency.[6]

Harvey and Drolet suggest that the eight empowerment principles be used to build strong, powerful people in a positive organizational climate.

I make every possible effort to apply and use these principles to empower my students, as we establish and maintain our own positive climate in the classroom. "Continuous improvement comes from empowering students to be self-motivated."[7]

When we revisit the classroom mission statement—"You will all Succeed!"[8]—we discuss its meaning and check for understanding as students give their interpretations. After a brief discussion, I give them a practical way to be successful in our classroom by participating in classroom jobs. As a starting point, we read the list of classroom jobs that previous classes have developed.

Figure 3.5. Force field analysis.

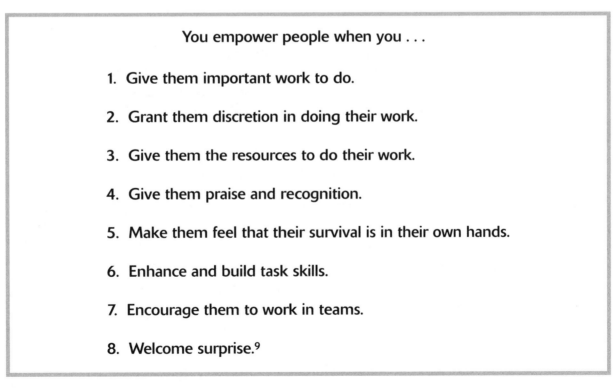

Table 3.1. Principles of Empowerment. Source: Thomas R. Harvey and Bonita Drolet, *Building Teams, Building People:* Technomic Publishing (now Landam MD: Scarecrow Press/Technomic Books), 1994, 127. Used with permission.

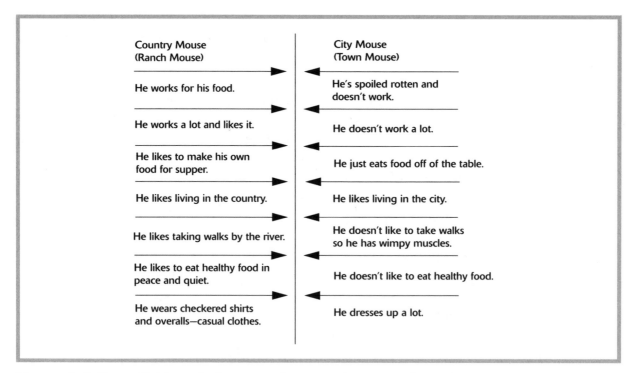

Figure 3.6. Force field analysis comparing two characters in a story.

Then I ask volunteers to role-play their own interpretations of each job description that I read aloud. Fellow classmates have to guess the job titles from the clues and charades. It is a fun way to introduce and practice the duties of each job. The student who guesses the correct job picks up the sign and puts that job title around the actor's neck. (I prepare the job-title yarn necklaces and signs beforehand.) When necessary, I interject information to clear up any misunderstanding of the required duties of each job.

We start with the jobs they have just role-played, because these offer a fresh point of reference. The Special Helper for the day is the first option in our classroom job chart. (Beforehand, I write each child's name on a 3 × 5 card and randomly organize them into a stack.) The first student whose name is pulled from the top of the stack is given the opportunity to accept the job. The child can also "pass" on that job by saying "No, thank you." Her card is then placed on the bottom of the stack. If her card comes up again, she will be reconsidered for any subsequent jobs. When someone accepts the responsibility of the Special Helper, I hand over the stack of name cards to that student. Once again I review the class rules about how to listen and wait for their turn to be chosen. The Special Helper assigns the remaining daily jobs to volunteers as their cards are pulled from the front and placed next to the job title card in the job chart. While the Special Helper is assigning classroom jobs like Classroom Librarian, Trash Inspector, Light Monitor, and Line Leader, I am able to take the attendance from the sign-in graph and count the number of lunches to be ordered on the other graph. We finish our tasks around the same time, and he or she takes the attendance sheet to the office. The children anticipate and enjoy being empowered to do the classroom jobs. An additional benefit of the job chart is that the students must frequently associate new names and faces. We learn each other's names much more quickly.

One of the jobs that requires a weekly commitment is that of group leader. This leadership role is passed around to every member of a four-student group, so that each student has the opportunity to learn and practice leadership skills one week of every month. The job description includes passing out and collecting papers, returning the group's work to their designated shelves, passing out and putting away math manipulatives, getting scissors and glue sticks, and sharpening pencils for the students in their group. Basically, their jobs are designed to meet the needs of their group. (Later in the year, the group leaders requested an assistant in their group to help with the responsibilities. The children voted and the group needs were divided.)

If the first group leader has a problem with someone in his or her group, I stop the activity and gather everyone on the open carpeted area to discuss the problem and find workable solutions. One quality tool I find useful to help students solve their own problems is the issue bin.

Issue Bin

"The issue bin is yet another tool that provides an effective process that allows everyone—students and teachers—to get all the cards on the table."[10] It can easily be made in minutes on a piece of chart paper, with the title "Issue Bin" written at the top with a marker and taped to the front white board.

The group leader is asked to report about his group's problem *without* mentioning specific names. (The purpose of the class meeting is to focus on the issue, not to embarrass or verbally attack each other.) After the group leader explains the problem and expresses the frustrations he is feeling, I ask the children to help me sum it up in one sentence. Volunteers are chosen by the Special Helper to help sound out and spell the words in the sentence as I write it on the chart paper. The children brainstorm possible solutions to help the frustrated group leader. One child, for instance, might suggest the group leader needs someone else in his group to help him. Every group leader then picks a helper to share the responsibility of meeting their group's needs. Our first problem in the issue bin is then checked off, signifying that we can work together to find a solution. I also draw a happy face next to the sentence to symbolize a happy ending.

The issue bin chart is set aside for further use. The first time we do this, I model how to write the issue on the chart. Next time, the recording job will be assigned to the Special Helper. He or she updates it when ideas and concerns pop up as we practice classroom routines and procedures. Issues that arise from incidents that take place outside of the classroom can also be listed on the issue bin chart. As a class, we discuss possible solutions to the problem(s). The positive solutions are written on a large piece of construction paper. Every student signs his or her name, including the teacher, to demonstrate agreement and willingness to participate. It is then placed in the classroom as a visual reminder.

The following section describes some of the solutions that have been generated using the issue bin as a quality tool.

Issue-Driven Classroom Jobs

Throughout the year, other classroom jobs are added or deleted when there is a specific need or purpose. When we studied meteorology, our class voted to have a classroom meteorologist go outside to check the thermometer, rain gauge, weather vane, anemometer, and barometer and report the cloud types in the sky. The data were collected and reported back to the class. The children wrote daily about the weather changes in their weather journals.

When we have a behavior problem in line, we put it on the issue bin chart and discuss the problem when we return to the classroom. We focus on the problem, *not* on the person who causes the incident. (This person writes an apology note and gives it to the offended classmate. This usually settles the problem privately without causing humiliation.) We brainstorm ways to improve our hallway behavior. Data are gathered and graphed using sticky dots to view our progress toward continuous improvement.

Individual student issues requiring a report to the principal and to parents are written on a form I have modified (Figure 3.7) from the problem-solving worksheet created by Mrs. Chronicle, a third-grade teacher at Central Elementary School in Linden, Michigan.

Some other classroom jobs were developed from issue bin discussions:

1. The Safety Inspector checks for untied shoelaces, counts the students, and is the last student in line after the recess bell rings.

2. The Quiet Inspector walks alongside the class line and uses a quiet signal (index finger next to the lips) to remind each child to be quiet as they walk in the hallway.

3. The Student Referee officiates recess basketball games.

The following stories demonstrate how the students were able to identify an issue and work through the process to bring about conflict resolution.

Two children argued for the last place in line for a couple of days as the class was lining up outside after recess. Some of their classmates brought it to my attention immediately as I walked down the sidewalk to greet them. They suggested that I call a class meeting. It was a situation that could not wait to be written on the issue bin chart inside our classroom. I called a class meeting, and we sat in a circle out on the playground. After a brief discussion, one of the children suggested we create another job, called Safety Inspector. The Safety Inspector would always be the last person in line, and would make sure everyone ahead of him or her arrived in the classroom safely.

I Can Think for Myself!

Name _____

Date _____

Draw an illustration:

Describe your problem:

What happened?_____

_____

_____

My face looked like this:

I felt _____ because _____

_____

Figure 3.7. Problem-solving worksheet.

I made this choice: _____

_____

_____

Some better choices I can make next time are:

1. _____

2. _____

3. _____

Draw an illustration of what you will do next time:

Next time I will _____

_____

_____

Student signature _____ Date _____

Parent signature _____ Date _____

Please review and return this signed form by tomorrow.

Figure 3.7. Continued.

Later in the year, a job was established that was needed to help monitor peer behavior. It was the students' suggestion to create the position of basketball referee during recess basketball games. This job was established after some problems occurred during morning recesses. Teams of five or more players ended up in daily fights at recess. This issue was placed in the issue bin. The students brainstormed suggestions, and we had a class discussion. Since students from another teacher's second grade were also involved, I told the students I would speak to that teacher after school. We discussed the problems, and he suggested we have teams of two players each.

I reported this back to the class the next day. The students tried this and still had some fights. We returned the issue to the issue bin and again brainstormed possible solutions. A child suggested creating the position of referee to monitor behavior during the game, like in professional basketball. The following guidelines for this position all came from students:

1. The position must last for a week.

2. The referee carries a clipboard to write down mutually agreed upon rules and team members before the game starts.

3. Each player must sign under the established rules before they are allowed to play.

4. The referee cannot play in the game.

5. The referee must carry the ball and clipboard out and back in again.

The suggestions were made by students, which empowered them to monitor their own behavior. The recess aides intervened only when necessary. I rarely had to get involved. If they could not solve the problems, the basketball games were suspended for a day or two until their emotions calmed down.

I am amazed at the positive effects and changes that empowerment makes on some less self-managed students from the beginning of the year to the end. Over time, and with much patience intertwined with consistent practice and positive reinforcement, many of these students become the best Quiet Inspectors, Safety Inspectors, and Student Referees. The expectation of behavior improvement produces an outcome of better self-control and management: "the more students practice their own problem solving, the more empowered they become thus leading to greater self-confidence and sense of responsibility for their own behavior."[11] Our classroom system provides daily opportunities to develop leadership skills in one of the supervisory roles. I am the encouraging facilitator of their roles and the supporter of their leadership positions.

The issue bin process is well worth the time it takes to work our way to an acceptable solution. It actually saves time as the year progresses because we are learning to continuously improve our behavior.

Plus Delta Chart

The Plus Delta chart is the final tool I will discuss in this chapter. It is another quality tool that I use often to evaluate the end of a day, a field trip, the end of a unit, and so on. I not only lead the discussion, but also record student volunteers' ideas and comments. Often the areas in which we need to improve (the delta column) are placed on the issue bin chart. I make mental notes to repeat what went well (the plus column) to ensure success when I plan other activities.[12] Figure 3.8 lists the ideas from the Plus Delta chart after one of our second- and third-grade writing experiences.

In summary, we continue to focus daily on the aim—"Maintain enthusiasm while increasing learning"[13]—for constancy of purpose. The students and I establish routines and set and modify our rules, using the fishbone and force field analysis and by revisiting the issue bin. The day spent together is often evaluated with the Plus Delta chart. Our community of learners flourishes while building positive relationships. Trust is nourished in our classroom system, and students feel valued, safe, and empowered within the structured routines and procedures. However, the children experience creativity within the structure. Within the scope of meaningful instruction, students can expect to have similar, but creative spelling lessons and activities each morning. Chap-

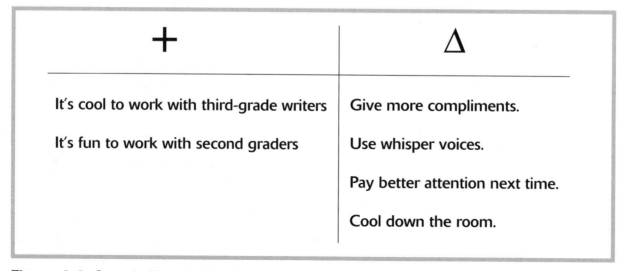

+	Δ
It's cool to work with third-grade writers	Give more compliments.
It's fun to work with second graders	Use whisper voices.
	Pay better attention next time.
	Cool down the room.

Figure 3.8. Sample Plus Delta chart.

ter 4 will thoroughly describe the successful spelling program I use each week with supporting data documenting continuous improvement in the classroom system.

Notes

1. Helio Gomes, *Quality Quotes* (Milwaukee, WI: ASQC Quality Press, 1996), 132.
2. Margaret Byrnes and Robert Cornesky, *Quality Fusion* (Port Orange, FL: Cornesky & Associates, 1994) 33.
3. Elizabeth Rike, *Language Arts Learning Experiences* (Portales, NM: Quality Education Association, 1998).
4. Nikos Kazantzakis, *A 3rd Serving of Chicken Soup for the Soul* (Deerfield Beach, FL: Health Communications, 1996), 113.
5. Thomas R. Harvey and Bonita Drolet, *Building Teams, Building People* (Lancaster, PA: Scarecrow Press/Technomic Books, 1994), 125.
6. Ibid., 127.
7. Margaret Byrnes, Robert Cornesky and Lawrence Byrnes, *The Quality Teacher* (Bunnell, FL: Cornesky & Associates, 1992), 184.
8. Harry Wong, *The First Days of School* (Sunnyvale, CA: Harry K. Wong Publications, 1991), 48.
9. Harvey and Drolet, *Building Teams, Building People*, 127.
10. Elaine McClanahan and Carolyn Wicks, *Future Force* (Chino Hills, CA: PACT Publishing, 1993), 36.
11. Byrnes and Cornesky, *Quality Fusion*, 52.
12. McClanahan and Wicks, *Future Force*, 38–39.
13. Lee Jenkins, *Improving Student Learning* (Milwaukee, WI: ASQ Quality Press, 1997), 115.

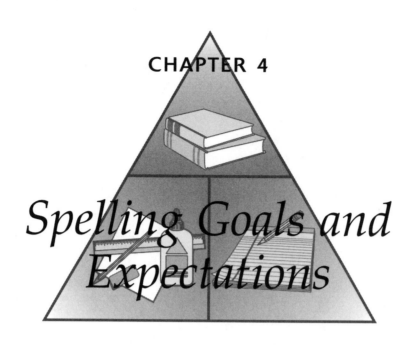

CHAPTER 4

Spelling Goals and Expectations

"Spelling is a cognitive act that requires the coordination of several sources of knowledge."

GRAHAM & MILLER, 1979;

SIMON & SIMON, 1973;

TEMPLETON, 1986;

WONG, 1986[1]

The purpose of this chapter is to give detailed explanations of my spelling program, and the supporting data that document five years of continuous improvement in the classroom system. Many scatter diagrams with student-overlay graphs, class run charts, histographs, and yearly comparison graphs are included.

I modify my weekly instructional practices according to gathered data. The additional input of California's smaller class size in the primary grades has significantly influenced my classroom system. The last three years of data support this fact. Over the last five years, my students have continuously improved because I use data to influence the way I teach. Without data, teachers speak of luck—"I had a great class this year." This statement implies that next year's class will return to the norm, and there is no expectation that each year's class will continually improve.

The school district in which I am employed has chosen the first one thousand high-frequency words,[2] compiled by Rebecca Sitton, as our focus words for spelling instruction. My responsibility as a second-grade teacher is to review the first one hundred and teach the second one hundred words throughout the whole year (Figure 4.1). The spelling goal for my students is to learn to spell these first two hundred words by the end the school year.

The lists of two hundred words are given to the parents at Back-to-School Night, when I present an in-depth explanation of my program. I encourage the parents to refer to these words as they help their children at home throughout the year. I explain to the parents that each week the students will practice these words within the context of meaningful sentences or phrases borrowed from second-grade core literature, poems, and songs, rather than in the typical vertical list format. The students must learn how to read the words and know the meaning of the words before they can be expected to spell them correctly.

Why is it important to learn how to spell high-frequency words correctly at an early age? High-frequency words are used for daily communication purposes by adults. Many of the high-frequency words cannot be easily sounded out, so young spellers must rely on visual strategies to learn the letter patterns. Often young spellers try to draw on their phonemic understanding to represent the sounds of the letters. They produce invented spellings that are not necessarily the standard spelling of the high-frequency words. "Spelling is a process drawing sometimes on visual memory and sometimes also on phonemic understanding," according to a qualitative study by Treiman in 1993.[3]

The following has consistently proven to be successful with students. The data will substantiate this claim later in the chapter.

Spelling Is Learned in Chunks of Text

We practice our spelling song, poem, or sentences right after our class opening and job chart assignments each morning. The first spelling song is the basis for many more lessons during the first week of school. Daily, beginning on

First 100 Spelling Words			Second 100 Spelling Words		
1. a	36. into	71. the	1. also	36. great	71. say
2. about	37. is	72. their	2. around	37. help	72. school
3. after	38. it	73. them	3. again	38. here	73. set
4. all	39. its	74. then	4. air	39. home	74. should
5. an	40. just	75. there	5. along	40. house	75. show
6. and	41. know	76. these	6. always	41. important	76. small
7. are	42. like	77. they	7. another	42. keep	77. something
8. as	43. little	78. this	8. any	43. large	78. sound
9. at	44. long	79. time	9. asked	44. last	79. still
10. be	45. made	80. to	10. away	45. left	80. such
11. been	46. make	81. two	11. back	46. line	81. take
12. but	47. many	82. up	12. because	47. look	82. tell
13. buy	48. may	83. use	13. below	48. man	83. think
14. called	49. more	84. very	14. between	49. me	84. those
15. can	50. most	85. was	15. big	50. men	85. thought
16. could	51. my	86. water	16. both	51. might	86. three
17. did	52. no	84. way	17. came	52. much	84. through
18. do	53. not	88. we	18. children	53. must	88. together
19. down	54. now	89. were	19. come	54. name	89. too
20. each	55. of	90. what	20. day	55. never	90. under
21. find	56. on	91. when	21. different	56. new	91. until
22. first	57. one	92. where	22. does	57. next	92. us
23. for	58. only	93. which	23. don't	58. number	93. want
24. from	59. or	94. who	24. end	59. off	94. well
25. had	60. other	95. will	25. even	60. often	95. went
26. has	61. out	96. with	26. every	61. old	96. while
27. have	62. over	97. words	27. few	62. our	97. why
28. he	63. people	98. would	28. food	63. own	98. work
29. her	64. said	99. you	29. form	64. part	99. world
30. him	65. see	100. your	30. found	65. place	100. write
31. his	66. she		31. get	66. put	
32. how	67. so		32. give	67. read	
33. I	68. some		33. go	68. right	
34. if	69. than		34. going	69. same	
35. in	70. that		35. good	70. saw	

Figure 4.1. First and second high-frequency word lists. Source: Rebecca Sitton's Spelling Sourcebook 2 Series, Copyright©1997, Egger Publishing, Inc., pg. 140–142. Toll-free 888-937-7355. Used with permission.

Monday, there will be a different focus on the song and a creative way to practice it. This way, the students will know it well by Friday. The tune sounds similar to a military cadence. The high-frequency words are in italics.

> "*I will always do my* best.
> *I can* handle *any* test.
> Learning *is* fun *at my school*.
> I'll control myself *and* obey *the* rules."

The expectations are modified for students struggling with spelling. Some students may be expected to learn only the high-frequency words in the first phrase, adding more phrases as their confidence and ability increases.

Weekly Schedule and Lesson Plans

Typical Monday Schedule

Our class spends more time in spelling activities on Monday mornings than during the rest of the week. This is a time to introduce a new group of words and a new application, while celebrating newly acquired words from the previous week and correctly practicing words that confused us and were recorded in the spelling folders.

Every Friday a new spelling song, poem, or group of sentences is introduced in the weekly homework packet, accompanied by several spelling-related activities suitable for home practice. The packets are ready each Friday morning because parents indicated on surveys that they wanted to document their children's reading experiences over the weekend, and to help them prepare for the upcoming week's learning experiences in spelling. Homework for the week goes home on Friday and is returned the following Friday. Some students come to school on Monday morning already familiar with the spelling text.

The spelling song is written on the board with some of the words—such as nouns, verbs or adjectives—missing, as in this example:

> I will always do my best.
> I can handle any _____.
> Learning is _____ at my _____.
> I'll control myself and obey _____ _____.

The students brainstorm other words that would make this song make sense. The purpose of the exercise is to use innovation to build comprehension and new vocabulary. Here is another possible arrangement of words which make the song make sense, but do not rhyme:

> I will always do my best
> I can handle any <u>chore</u>.
> Learning is fun at my <u>house</u>.
> I'll control myself and obey *my parents*.

The students must illustrate the song so it matches the words to demonstrate understanding of the text. In the example, the only high-frequency word that changed was *school*. The students received reinforcement on the spelling of several high-frequency words: *I, will, always, do, my, can, any, is, at, and*. Those words are the ones they must know by Friday. When they understand that those words are the only words they are responsible to learn that week, the spelling song doesn't seem so overwhelming. Most students will be able to correctly spell each word by Friday. They will at least be able to spell all the consonants in all the words by Friday, because the consonants are much easier to hear. The more children are exposed to a difficult word—reading it, writing it, practicing it in spelling games—the more quickly they learn to spell it.

Dictated High-Frequency Word Practice

In this lesson I cover up the spelling song and dictate just the high-frequency words by segmenting the sounds, slowly sounding out each phoneme. The children write down the sounds they hear. I say something to this effect: "Slowly trap the sound your mouth is forming or that you hear in your head with your fingers and put it into your pencil. Quickly write it down before it floats away!" Since many high-frequency words are difficult to sound out letter by letter, the visual letter patterns have to be memorized. We call those words "the ones that do not play fair." The words that do "play fair"—such as *I, will, can, is, at, and*—are described as "soundable" spelling words. Other times I dictate ten more words off the list and ask the students to give advice on how to help one of their friends improve in spelling.

After we correct the dictated words together, I have the students look for and underline all of the high-frequency words on copies of the first and second hundred-word lists. This activity helps the students again see the correct form of the word, and it is reinforced into their memory. These word lists can be taken home weekly to practice the underlined high-frequency words.

Spelling Folders and Student-Made Bar Graphs

In a discussion with a fellow district teacher, I learned that her intermediate students graph their own spelling results each week. At the time, I made computer-generated student line graphs and gave them to the students. In addition, I decided to allow my second graders to color in their own progress on grid paper to make a bar graph. This has proven to be a very successful learning experience that integrates math and spelling. I set up the process in this way:

Each Monday morning we revisit the previous week's assessment of fourteen random words. This is already filed in their legal-sized personal spelling folder from the prior Thursday's test. When the students open their spelling folders, they find a sheet of one-inch grid paper taped to the top of the folder on the left side. Each column is dated with the previous Thursday's assessment date. The total amount of correct high-frequency words is colored in the grid from the bottom up, with one square representing one word correct. For example, if a child scored nine out of fourteen words correct, she colors in nine squares (Figure 4.2). Then the student matches the correct spelling words from the test to the high-frequency-word lists taped at the top of the right side of her folder. Each correct word is colored in with a colored pencil or regular pencil. The children enjoy seeing the gradual accumulation of correctly spelled words as the high-frequency word lists begin to fill up with color. Both the bar graph and the colored-in word lists become visual reminders each week of their progress. It is extremely important for children to experience success often as they are attempting to learn.

The other incorrect words are practiced in a spelling/handwriting book compiled by another teacher colleague. The student practices each word correctly two times next to the correct spelling of the word. She then puts the newly practiced spelling words into complete sentences, using the lined page that follows the page for individual word practice. A parent volunteer writes the word at the beginning of the line to give the student less chance of copying the word incorrectly and practicing the wrong spelling. Practicing the correct spelling and placing it in a meaningful sentence helps to reinforce the standard spelling of the word. This kind of repetition seems to help students memorize the words more quickly.

As an old saying goes, "It takes ten rights to correct one wrong." When I was a private piano instructor for approximately eight years, my students were able to learn one difficult measure of music by practicing that particular measure ten to fifteen times in a row. Otherwise that troublesome measure always tripped the student up, no matter how many times he started the song over. Once the student focused on correct repetitions of the troublesome measure or difficult fingering pattern, that part became easier to play

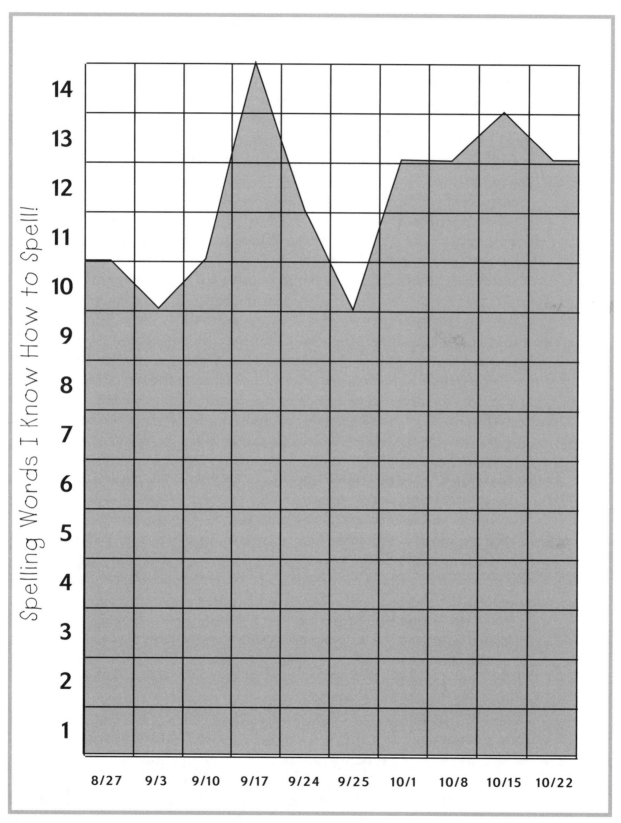

Figure 4.2. Student's bar graph of spelling scores.

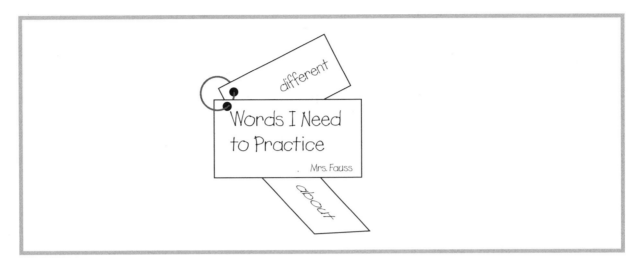

Figure 4.3. Word ring.

without "tripping over it." Then the students would rerun that particular phrase (like rerunning a sentence in reading) from the beginning and glide through it smoothly. Progress was made much more quickly, and the student didn't lose his enthusiasm for learning the song. Small successes resulted in a big reward when the student played the whole song well.

The less familiar words are also copied onto 3 × 5 cards that have been cut into fourths and hole-punched. These cards are placed on a metal ring that can open and latch (Figure 4.3). Each word is taken off as soon as the student can spell it without difficulty and "challenges" me with the word. This takes place any time the child believes the correct spelling of the word is memorized. If the student can recite the correct spelling of the word without looking, finger-spell it in sign language, and use it correctly in a sentence, I tear it off the ring and throw it in the trash. The child and I celebrate! Keeping a word ring empty seems to motivate the students.

Typical Tuesday Schedule

We sing the song together again. I print out a modified cloze task, in which I remove all of the vowels from the song (Figure 4.4). The students can only see consonants and a line holding the spot where the vowels need to be written. We have a lesson focused on consonants—what they are, what they are not. Since consonants are easier to learn at first, we clap all the consonants as we say the alphabet. Every time we come to a vowel we purposely miss our hands and form a silent clap. I find out who knows the difference between a vowel and a consonant quickly in this activity. Then I give each student two

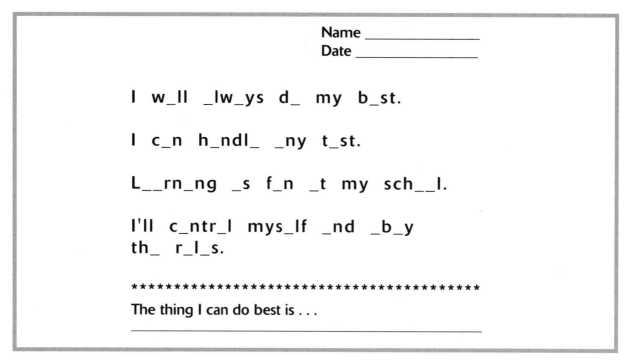

Figure 4.4. Modified cloze task with vowels removed.

sentence strips taped together. They are instructed to write down only the consonants using capital letters. As an extension, they write all the consonants again in alphabetical order using lower-case letters on the back side. I find out who needs more practice with upper-case and lower-case letter formation. The children then complete the spelling song modified cloze activity. This type of spelling practice page seems to help students to really focus on the beginning, middle, and end of the words.

Typical Wednesday Schedule

We review the song. I give the children a cut-and-paste job to do. One piece of paper has all the words randomly placed on the page. They cut and glue the words in the correct sequence onto the line below the correct typed-in phrase.

Typical Thursday Schedule

Every Thursday morning I give the students fourteen randomly chosen words from the first two hundred-word lists. One teacher colleague refers to ran-

Grade	Total Words	Words on Weekly Quiz
1	100	10
2	200	14
3	300	17
4	400	20
5	500	22
6	600	24
7 & 8	1000	32

Figure 4.5. High-frequency words by grade.[4]

domly chosen words or concepts as "preview/review" words or concepts. The number of words—fourteen—is based on the square root of the total amount of high-frequency spelling words. The square root of the total is an adequate sample. It assesses a large sample of words at one time without overwhelming the students. The same formula applies to other grades (Figure 4.5). "[Dr. Deming's] theory was to measure the square root of the total. A random number table was created so that all teachers could recycle spelling words throughout the first eight grades."

Another way to randomly choose the words is to have a student roll a two-sided die and a hundred-sided die simultaneously. The two-sided die chooses the hundred-word list and the other die chooses the word. Each spelling word is numbered on the spelling list charts. Class Action™ also offers a random number feature, Numble Jumble™.[5] (See ordering information from ASQ Quality Press in Appendix B). Students may gather fourteen numbers and then match the numbers to the words on the lists. It is rare that the words chosen randomly match the words we are working on that week in our spelling song, poem, or sentences. The students are not cramming for the weekly spelling test. The possibility of cramming must be removed in order for teachers to have accurate process data. The random test becomes an authentic assessment of their growth and retention of high-frequency words over the year, as opposed to soon-forgotten weekly crammed spelling words. Seeing the students consistently use the correct form of the word in their stories is a true application of information toward knowledge.

The students write their first attempt at the random spelling words with a fine-tip black marker on the left side of the paper, so I can gather an accurate sample before correction. The correct spellings of the words are practiced by finger-spelling in sign language, and written in colored or regular pencil on the right side of the paper as we discuss and correct them together.

Students enjoy leading their peers in finger-spelling in sign language at the front of the room.

On the other side of the spelling assessment paper, I photocopy another variation of the spelling song, poem, or sentences. This time I take out all of the consonants (Figure 4.6). The students write in all of the consonants. This activity immediately follows the whole-class random spelling assessment. It seems to help the students really focus on each word. By this time in the week, most of the children have the song, poem, or sentences memorized. (They not only visit it in our different class activities throughout the week, but also practice it in their homework each night.) If they need help remembering any of the words, I always have the song, poem, or sentences written on the white board or in a pocket chart at the front of the room.

Typical Friday Schedule

Each trimester I make a small booklet of twelve pages to be titled *My Book of Spelling Sentences*. The students copy the title from the board and and write their names on the front. Using a ruler the students draw lines upon which

---

Name _____
Date _____

Fill in all missing consonants in the spelling song.

I _i__ a__a__ _o __ _e__.

I _a_ _a___e a__ _e__.

_ea__i__ i_ _u_ a_ __ ___oo_.

I'__ _o___o_ ___e__ a__ o_e_ __e _u_e.

What is an important rule to keep while you
are playing at recess?

_____

Figure 4.6. Modified cloze task with consonants removed.

they write each spelling song, poem, and sentence. After it is copied, they draw an illustration on the page in a one- or two-inch square. Students enjoy being able to read this collection of text and take pride in being able to spell most of the high-frequency words. They also review by reading previous sentences before they add the new one each week. At the end of the trimester, the booklet is read and shared with our kindergarten pals and families.

After everyone is finished writing the song in their booklets, I erase it from the board. I hand out another copy of the spelling song, but this time I have printed only the first letter of each high-frequency word, leaving the correct amount of blank lines to finish the word (Figure 4.7). The children write the spelling song as I sing it to them in a dictation activity. Many students join me in singing the song as they write it. When the front side of the spelling song, poem, or sentences is completed, the children who are capable write the whole dictation without any printed structure, using auditory cues, on the blank back side of the paper. Most of the students can write all of the words correctly, even though they are only responsible for the high-frequency words.

Spelling Extension Ideas

I am gleaning much new learning from Dr. Donald Bear's *Words Their Way*. This book presents his research and work in developmental spelling and how it correlates to the student's writing and reading ability. Patricia Cunningham's work in *Making Words* provides helpful fun activities in word study.

Students learn how to spell words of their choice in *My Important Word Book*. An adult writes the correct spelling of the word on the first short line. Students practice the word five times, then write it into a sentence and draw an illustration. Another open-ended spelling activity is practicing the weekly phonogram(s) from the spelling song, poem, or sentences and compiling each page in a book. (See Appendix A.)

Weekly Tabulation and Graphing of Student Data

On Thursday afternoons I enter every child's correct total of words from the random spelling test onto the spreadsheet, usually in less than ten minutes. The data are automatically saved into each student's file and organized into a "visual grade book." The software does all the graphing. I enter data onto the spreadsheet as teachers have done for years on record sheets or grade books.

Name_____

Date_____

I w___ a_____ d_ m_ best.

I c__ handle a__ test.

Learning i_ fun a_ m_ s_____.

I'll control myself a__ obey
th_ rules.

Draw a picture of something you do to follow our
classroom rules:

Figure 4.7. Spelling dictation page.

The monitoring and assessment of weekly process data in this book would not have been possible without the versatile Class Action™ software, developed in 1997. (Ordering information can be found in Appendix B.) It can create scatter diagrams for monitoring individual students in classroom systems like no other software program currently available.

Speaking from experience, I have learned to appreciate the value of this time-saving software program. The graphs help me to gain insight about my students. When studying a scatter diagram with upper and lower control lines, I can pinpoint exactly who and where a student is within our classroom system by merely moving the mouse, pointing the arrow, and clicking on that dot. The student's name appears in the lower left corner of the screen. In less than a second, I can tell if a student is functioning well within my current classroom system or needs special assignments adapted specifically to his or her needs. As I watch student performance on random (preview/review) weekly assessments, I can determine if there is gradual growth in understanding, or if I should ask special services to intervene for this child with strategies beyond my expertise or training.

There are several options for displaying the week's data:

1. Whole-class scatter diagram for the teacher to study (Figure 4.8). This can also be printed out with a different color dot for students sorted by gender, ethnicity, or any other teacher-selected variable.

2. Whole-class run chart for the class to study (Figure 4.9).

3. Whole-class histogram for the teacher to study (Figures 4.10). For example, a separate graph can be printed for each trimester or quarter. The teacher can set the period of time to be studied.

4. Individual student run chart with weekly data scores (Figure 4.11).

5. Student run charts overlaid onto class scatter diagrams with upper and lower control limits are helpful during parent conferences and SST and IEP meetings (Figure 4.12). The two outside lines set the perimeters of the classroom system. The middle (bold) student line graph indicates that he or she is functioning within the current classroom system. Students functioning at the upper-limit line or below the lower-limit line need special assignments.

Most importantly, each graph is helpful in gaining insight about a student's progress. It provides a clearer picture when trying to explain the child's progress to parents. The old saying "A picture is worth a thousand words" can easily be adjusted to "A graph is worth a thousand letter grades."

Each week I display the class run chart. The students and I study and discuss our weekly progress. The graphs show the students whether they "beat the computer or the computer beat them" in this imaginary competition. Actually, the weekly random sampling of words tests the effectiveness of my spelling instruction and acquisition of language from my reading program. I should be seeing gradual overall improvement as the year progresses. If my students are not making gradual progress over several weeks (usually seven consecutive weeks) of data collection, my teaching strategies must be changed to better meet their learning modalities.

Many of my teacher colleagues work hard and hope their students learn and improve, but do not gather data. It makes sense to get weekly feedback on whether or not the spelling instruction is being effective by observing student data. Weekly celebrations or problem-solving sessions are conducted after the process data are collected. The suggestions the students offer for

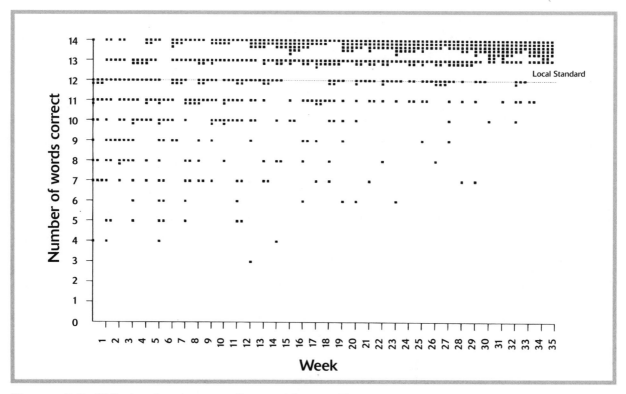

Figure 4.8. Whole-class scatter diagram for spelling scores.

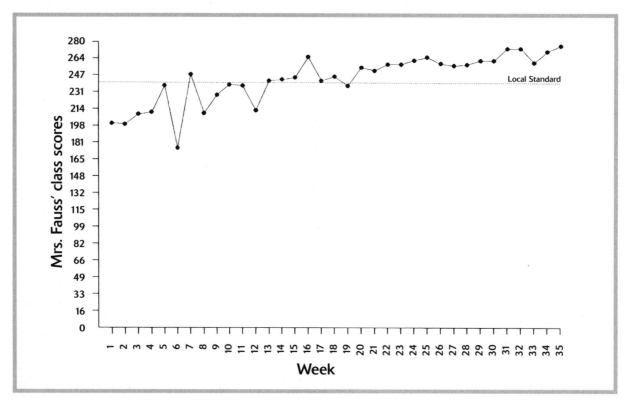

Figure 4.9. Class run chart for spelling scores.

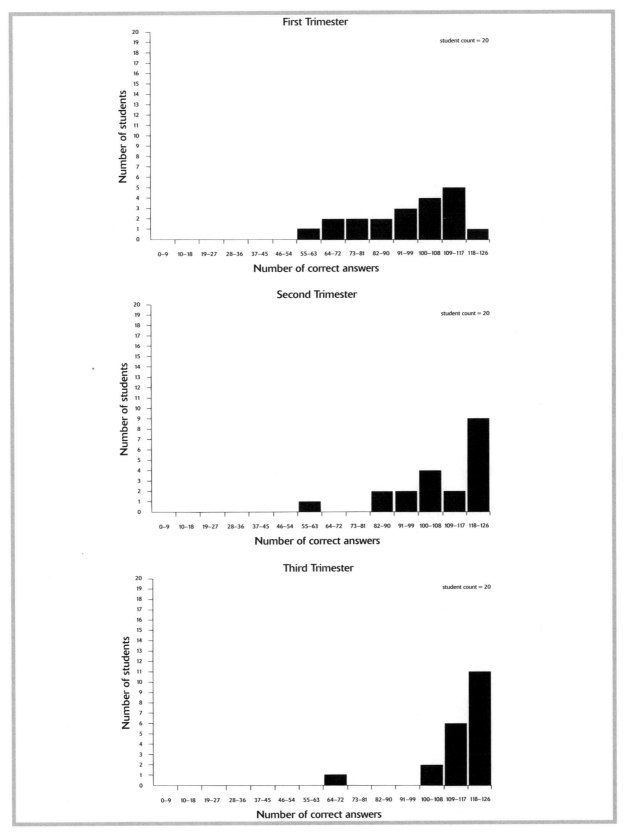

Figure 4.10. Histogram for spelling scores.

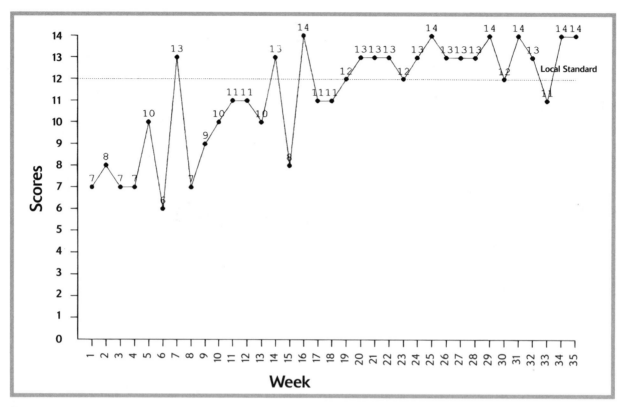

Figure 4.11 Student run chart for spelling scores.

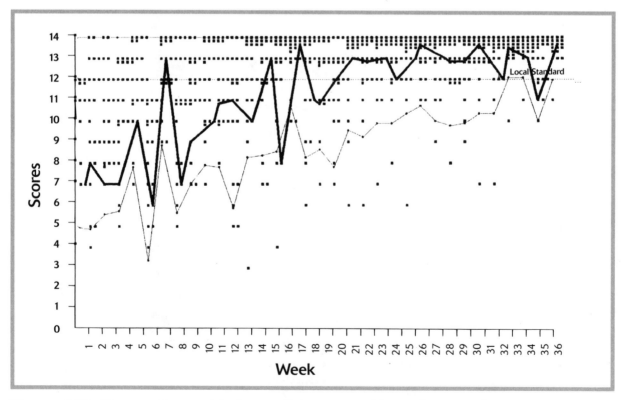

Figure 4.12 Class scatter matrix for spelling scores with student overlay.

spelling improvement are implemented in our current class system as much as possible, and we study the following week's data to see if the suggestions brought about improvement in our spelling scores and application to writing. The process data drives the instruction. Student feedback drives instruction. We, the classroom of learners, make informed decisions based on weekly data to improve our system.

Hoping Students Are Improving vs. Knowing Students Are Improving

Since 1994 I have been graphing student success with high-frequency words by using the weekly random selection sample of fourteen words from the first two hundred-word lists. I *know* my students are improving in spelling because I see gradual growth validated by the graphed data. I expect next year's class to outperform the prior year's classes as they have for the past five years.

Unfortunately, many teachers have not had access to data collection and graphing on a computer. They have a gut feeling their students are improving. (I don't know of a teacher anywhere who doesn't want his or her students to improve.) It's difficult to notice the whole class's growth from week to week, even if copious notes are kept on each child for comparison after each quarter or trimester. Most teachers do not celebrate weekly because they do not know they have something to celebrate. Computer software helps to make data collection manageable and less time-consuming. However, graphing data by plotting the points on graph paper and making a class line graph or a single student run chart is possible for teachers without access to the software. Either method lets teachers know if their students are making continuous improvement or not.

Class Spelling Data

Spelling Data for 1994–95

The 1994–95 class line graph is the first example that illustrates this fact. I was able to see growth in my class's high-frequency spelling words acquisition (Figure 4.13). I saved that graph from my first year of data collection, so I could compare it week by week with my new class's weekly progress during the 1995–96 school year (Figure 4.14). I was working toward continuous improvement in my spelling instruction.

Spelling Data for 1995–96

After the first random word test of the 1995–96 school year, I compared the data to that from 1994–95. The first thing I noticed was that the new class came into my room knowing 65 more high-frequency words than the previous class. The class of 1994–95 had a cumulative score of 152 correct words when they took their first random fourteen-word test, compared to the total of 217 for the class of 1995–96. The class of 1995–96 outperformed the class of 1994–95 in high-frequency spelling (Figure 4.15).

I learned to appreciate the scatter diagram in 1995–96. "So much of educational data masks over individual children, but the scatter diagram may prove to be the most powerful of the decision-making quality tools because every dot represents a child."[6] The growth of all my students was clearly shown on the 1995–96 scatter diagram (Figure 4.16). It validated that I was making correct decisions in regard to high-frequency spelling words instruction as the year progressed. My goal was to move from a wide range of scores the first week to a more compact dot configuration near the upper-right corner of the graph by the last week of school. I watched their weekly collective progress after each random fourteen-word test. As the weeks progressed, I noticed that the dots were in fact moving up. This told me that my students were improving in their acquisition of correct spelling words. Even the speller who struggled the most was making some progress over time. My classroom system was continuously improving in spelling with only a few small dips (from special causes) in scores. We celebrated every week after a spelling assessment. Who ever heard of celebrating spelling assessments each week?

Spelling Data for 1996–97

In the fall of 1996, California reduced the maximum class size for kindergarten through second grade from thirty-two students to just twenty. Although my 1996–97 class came in knowing fewer high-frequency words than the previous class of thirty-two, they made accelerated progress from the beginning of August to December. From the results data that year, I can only assume the lower class size made the difference.

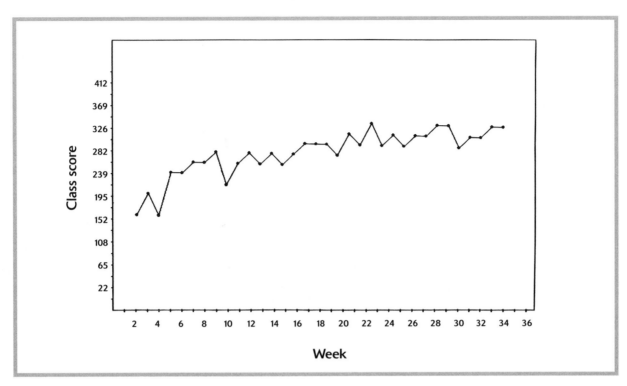

Figure 4.13. Class run chart for spelling scores, 1994–95.

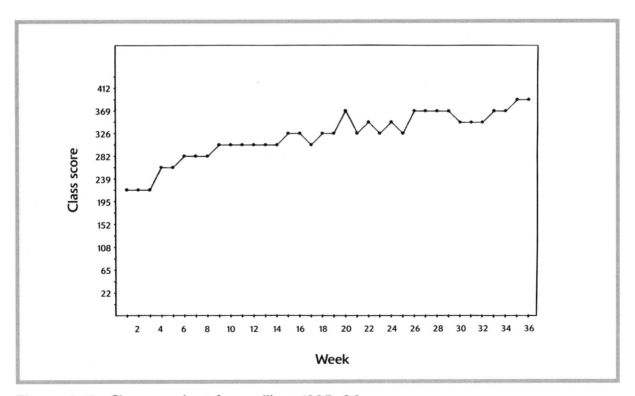

Figure 4.14. Class run chart for spelling, 1995–96.

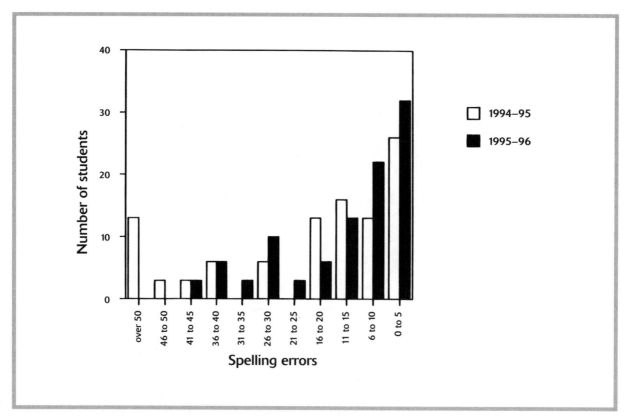

Figure 4.15. Two years of comparative data for spelling scores.

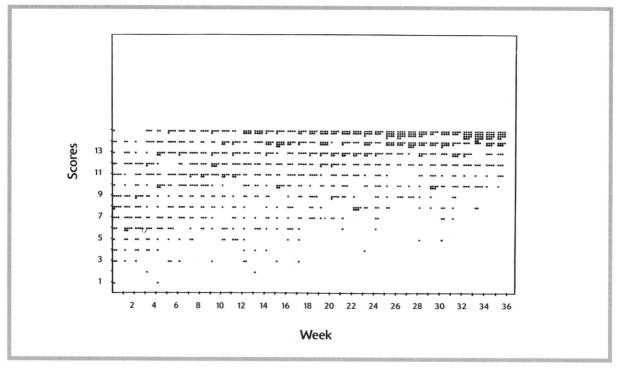

Figure 4.16. Class scatter diagram for spelling scores, 1995–96.

Spelling Data for 1997–98

After a few weeks of collecting weekly data during the new 1997–98 school year, I compared the number of high-frequency words my students knew to what my students knew at the same time the previous year. The new class came in knowing sixty-eight more words than the prior year's new second-grade students. Was it a coincidence that the previous year, 1996–97, was also the first year of smaller class sizes in California? I think not. According to the data I gathered, it seemed the lower class size had given first-grade teachers fewer students and more opportunities to prepare their twenty students for second grade.

I decided to take a copy of a graph that compared both years to the first staff meeting, to celebrate the wonderful job my first-grade colleagues had done in spelling preparation. This kind of public acknowledgment of a job well done from teacher to teacher had never happened in the school's five-year existence. I was the only one who had data to prove it. The data gave me the opportunity to affirm my hardworking first-grade colleagues. It was such a rewarding experience that I plan to compare data from year to year and find more opportunities to celebrate with my colleagues.

A week or two later, my students took the weekly fourteen-word test. As I reviewed the tests and input their scores into Class Action™, I noticed the students had scored lower than they had the previous four weeks. I was naturally concerned, as any caring teacher is when students do not perform well. The second week of school we had a lower cumulative score than the first week, but the third and fourth weeks we had improved our scores.

During the previous four years of collecting weekly class spelling data, I had never seen that drastic of a dip before in total words correct. (This may happen to your class sometime.) I immediately wanted to make some changes to "fix" the problem, but wasn't sure where to begin. However, I used my knowledge and not my emotions by studying the data. After analyzing the data more thoroughly, two factors emerged. First, ten out of fourteen words were difficult second-hundred words. Second, a student moved away earlier in the week who happened be a great speller. It was obvious that we, as a classroom of learners, had a lot of work to do to learn those ten words. This was an issue we worked through after we put it in the issue bin.

The point I am trying to make is, don't implement any drastic changes in the classroom system if this should happen to your students. Study more weeks of data—at least seven weeks in a row—before implementing whatever changes you and your students decide to try. The rationale is this:

Conservative statisticians say that seven weeks of collecting data after a change has been made is necessary to prove whether the growth is due to luck or improvement. Why seven weeks? Because statisticians want to be able to say there is less than a 1 percent chance the growth was caused by good luck.[7]

    If changes are implemented, watch the data carefully to see if the changes helped to improve your classroom system.

    After reviewing the high-frequency spelling words graph for the completed 1997–98 school year, it is obvious the decision not to significantly change the classroom system after the fifth-week spelling assessment was correct. During the sixth and eleventh weeks of school we had one more student move away and two new students join our class. After the eleventh-week random spelling assessment, our class only continued to improve their total of correct high-frequency spelling words (Figure 4.17). The 1997–98 class outperformed the 1996–97 class. Data for two years of class-size reduction had been gathered and compared.

    The control-chart scatter diagram with student overlay for Torre (Figure 4.18) clearly demonstrated that he was functioning above my current classroom structure in spelling achievement at the fourteenth week of school. When he received seven straight perfect scores in our weekly assessments, there was statistically less than a 1 percent chance that he would miss any of the first two hundred high-frequency words. Based on the data, I had to modify my instruction to meet his needs. Rather than test him on seventeen out of the first three hundred words, I decided to test him on twenty random high-frequency spelling words from the first four hundred-word lists. These words kept him challenged until the last four weeks of school. At that time he had scored twenty out of twenty for seven weeks, so I put him on the fifth and sixth hundred-word lists. He worked on twenty-five randomly selected high-frequency spelling words until the last week of school. He had already demonstrated to me he could read all one thousand high-frequency words off of the lists. I had to plan difficult spelling activities to keep him challenged each week. One challenge I gave him was the task of putting all six hundred words in alphabetical order. That kept him motivated for a day or two. He also consistently demonstrated correct spelling and usage of the first four hundred high-frequency words in his lengthy stories. He used his understanding of the high-frequency words (information) and applied them correctly in the stories he had written (knowledge).

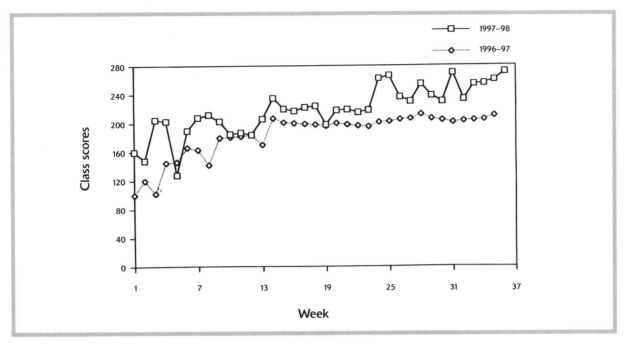

Figure 4.17. Class run charts for two years of class-size reduction.

Spelling Data for 1998–99

The data I have collected prove that my students have outperformed the previous years' classes. I attribute the continuous improvement to the addition of a kinesthetic modality spelling instruction strategy. My students and I practiced and learned finger-spellings in sign language. Each high-frequency word was spelled out using sign language. I also used some software with which the high-frequency words could be printed in sign language hand symbols for my students to translate back into the standard spellings. Every possible effort was made to include all learning modalities in my spelling instruction.

Comparative Data from the Annual District Assessments

Figure 4.19, which shows five years of comparative data (1994–99), demonstrates that my students have made fewer spelling errors each successive year

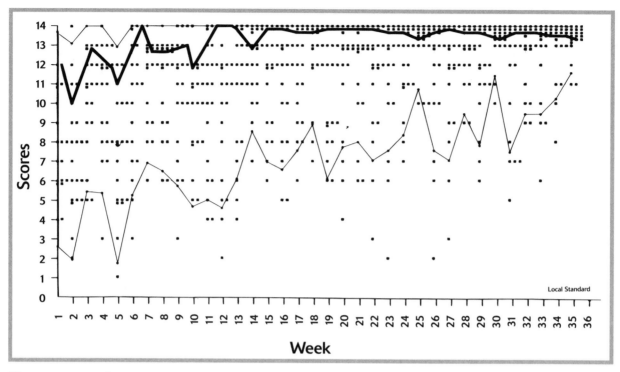

Figure 4.18. Class scatter matrix for spelling scores with student overlay.

during the last seven weeks of the year. The results data for 1996–97, 1997–98, and 1998–99 show my classroom system is going through continuous improvement. The 1998–99 class has outperformed the previous classes.

1996–97

At a district grade-level meeting, the second-grade teachers decided to test forty out of the two hundred high-frequency words. A child would exceed the district's benchmarks in spelling by achieving 37–40 correct. Our district standard was met when a child scored 30–36 words correct, and 0–29 words correct would be below standard. Later in the school year, grade-level comparative data was gathered throughout the district for 1996–97. The following graph displays my students' performance compared to the overall district performance in second-grade spelling (Figures 4.20). I attribute the difference to the fact that I know each and every week how my students are performing and can make timely adjustments in my instruction, rather than waiting until the end of the year when it's too late to do anything about it.

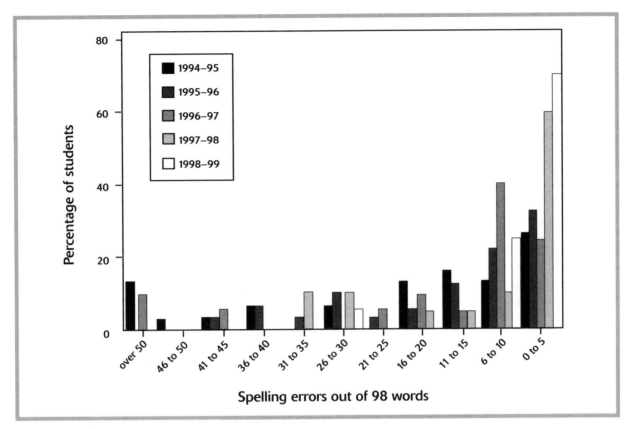

Figure 4.19. Five years of continuous improvement in spelling scores.

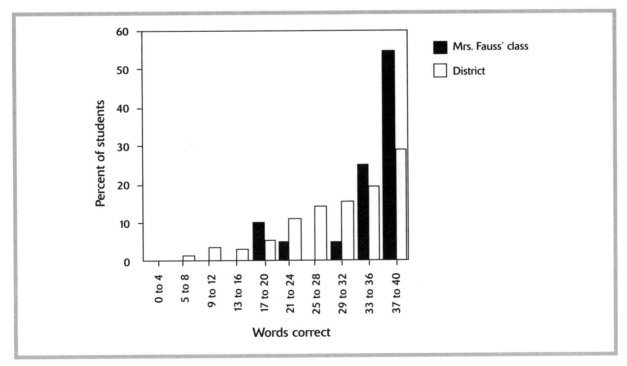

Figure 4.20. Scores for district spelling assessment, 1996–97.

1997–98

In order to meet the second-grade standard for our school district, students had to score at least 30–36 out of 40 high-frequency words correctly. Figure 4.21 shows that 90 percent of my students met our district's standard in spelling.

1998–99

Figures 4.22 and 4.23 compare the results data of all second graders in the district to that of my second-grade students. Ninety five percent of my students met or exceeded the district standard.

In summary, this chapter has covered spelling instruction in detail, with graphs displaying student, class, and district data. It is my hope that the reader will find the ideas useful while working through continuous improvement in the classroom system. My students' improvement in spelling is attributed to the fact that I know each and every week how individual students are progressing. By watching the data so closely, I can make informed decisions about changes in instruction to effectively meet the individual needs of my students (Figure 4.24). What I have learned this year, from the masters and from experts in various fields, has helped to improve my spelling instruction.

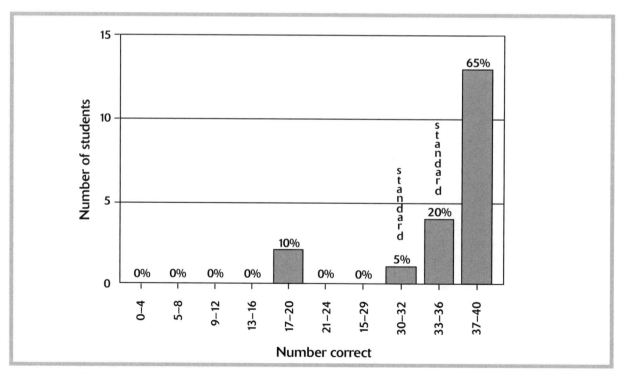

Figure 4.21. Mrs. Fauss' class' scores on district spelling assessment, 1997–98.

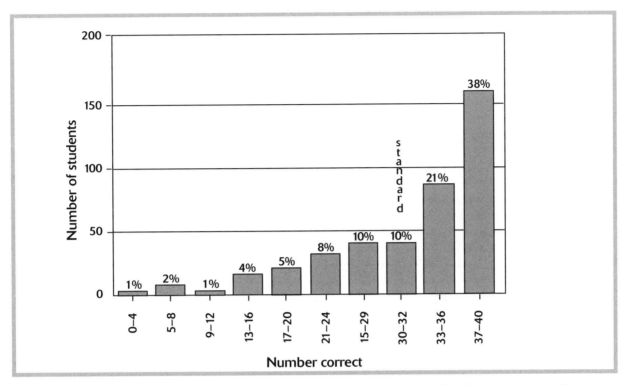

Figure 4.22. Overall scores on district assessment, 1997–98. Used with permission.

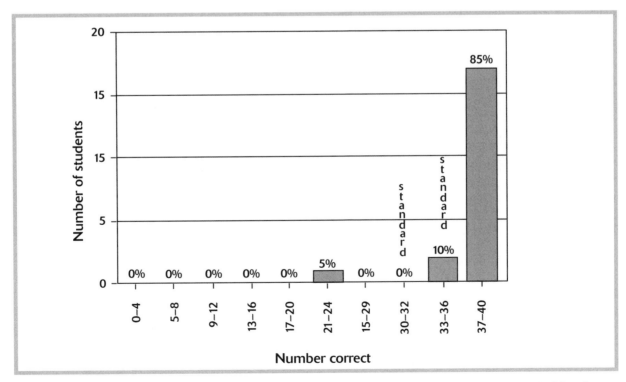

Figure 4.23. Mrs. Fauss' class scores on district spelling assessment, 1998–99. Used with permission.

Figure 4.24. More data, I need more data![8]

This book is designed to combine all of the components of "Our Classroom as a System" (chapter 1) so that students can demonstrate their learning in measurable data or information, and transfer that learning to more difficulty measured knowledge. This will impact their futures significantly. Students can demonstrate knowledge through writing assignments. Chapter 5 contains many examples, ideas, and exercises that provide more joyful writing experiences across the curriculum compatible to the aim: "Maintaining enthusiasm while increasing learning."[9]

Notes

1. Gladys Rosencrans, *The Spelling Book* (Newark, DE: International Reading Association, 1998), 16.
2. Rebecca Sitton, *Spelling Sourcebook 2 Series* (Scottsdale, AZ: Egger Publishing, 1997), 140–42.
3. Karin Dahl and Nancy Farnan, *Children's Writing, Perspectives from Research* (Newark, DE: International Reading Association, 1998), 62.

4. Lee Jenkins, *Applying Quality Principles in the Classroom* (Cedar Rapids, IA, 1995), 11.

5. Mike DeSilvio, *Class Action*™ (Miami, FL: Blackthorne Publishing Company, 1997).

6. Lee Jenkins, *Improving Student Learning* (Milwaukee, WI: ASQ Quality Press, 1997), 182.

7. Ibid., 72, 73.

8. *Clip Art*™ with caption added by Dan Flores, Enterprise School District. Used with permission.

9. Jenkins, *Applying Quality Principles in the Classroom*, 115.

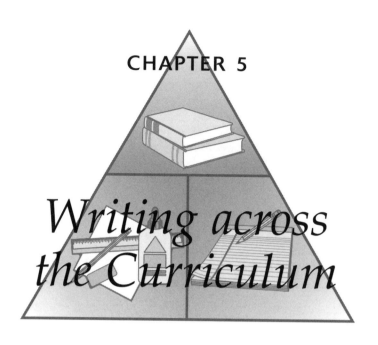

CHAPTER 5

Writing across the Curriculum

"Writing requires children to think about the sounds and meanings of spoken words, to observe the characteristics of printed words, and to form hypotheses about the relations between sounds and letters. All of these activities are of great value in helping children grasp the alphabetic nature of the English writing system."

TREIMAN[1]

The previous chapter focused on teaching spelling and gathering spelling data. The purpose of chapter 5 is to provide meaningful instruction when writing across the curriculum, focusing on the aim: "Maintain enthusiasm while increasing learning."[2] Transferring spelling into consistent application in writing poses a difficult challenge for every teacher. Spelling applies to writing as information applies to knowledge. One way a child can demonstrate under-standing of a concept, turning information into knowledge, is by explaining it in a writing assignment. Some spelling concepts are actually learned while writing.

"The errors children make as they write are neither random nor thought-less. When examined diagnostically, they reveal systematic application of the child's level of understanding," according to Buchana (1989), Gentry (1987), and Tarasoff (1990).[3] Primary students also need daily writing opportunities to build fluency. Through daily writing experiences, the primary teacher is preparing new second-grade students (supply) to continue as more advanced writers in third grade and beyond. Third-grade teachers are the customers the next year.

Writing every day is an expectation. The writing procedures listed below allow the teacher to constantly evaluate process data (stories in progress) to improve student writing in the classroom. Writing lessons in our classroom usually flow in this order:

1. Students make choices of topics or write from a stimulus involving the five senses, such as an experience, an educational video, or an event like a field trip or social activity.

2. Teacher and other student or adult volunteers edit while the story pro-gresses. Several mini writing lessons in structure and adding detail take place with individual students while everyone is writing. (Observations the teacher makes while working with the students often become a whole-class lesson to be taught the following day. The students continue on with the writing project with a focus on a new skill.)

3. When a student asks how to spell a word, the standard spelling of the word is written in her personal speller by an adult for the child to copy into her story.

4. Our third-grade writing coaches work with us using on selected pieces a six-point rubric.

5. After much revision, the student is ready to "publish" a story. She can choose to trace over the edited story with a felt pen, or to type it up on the classroom computer or in the computer lab. It is then attached to the artwork with tape or glue.

6. Students are provided weekly opportunities to read their stories to at least one of the people in the following list: fellow classmates, kinder-garten, third-, fourth-, or fifth-grade buddies, office personnel, the prin-cipal, the custodians, cooks, classroom visitors, and so on.

7. The "published" piece is displayed on each student's personal bulletin board in the classroom or on the second/third-grade joint bulletin board in the hall.

Writer's Folders: Writer's Choice

I give the students time to write personal stories from past and current experiences during a time we call "Writer's Folders." The important part of Writer's Folders time is that students can choose to write about anything they want. I often have volunteers in the classroom at this time to assist the students by discussing possible ways to illustrate an idea to write, helping some students get started.

As the children write, some of the volunteers ask me if they should help with spelling or allow the students to use inventive spelling throughout the whole story. The following passage provides a solution for this dilemma, which we teachers face daily:

A common theory held by many teachers is that they should not help a student with spelling while he or she is writing a first draft. They tell the student to do his or her best; editing comes later. The theory is that attention paid to spelling in the first draft will cause the young writer to lose creativity and productivity. According to Dr. Deming only one example contrary to this theory would be necessary to demand its revision. Only one child is needed whose writing creativity is damaged and productivity lessened by a teacher's refusal to help with spelling during the writing of a first draft. Likely every teacher knows of a perfectionist child who needs to know spelling right now or both creativity and production are lessened. Therefore the theory of spelling assistance must be revised. Perhaps an additional theory should be, 'some children will write more creatively and produce more text when they can attend to spelling during the first draft.'[4]

As the students write, I observe that they want to know how to spell words correctly. The students are expected to write correctly the high-frequency words we are currently learning. They often refer to Rebecca Sitton's high-frequency word lists and underline the word they need, so it will be easier to find next time.[5] The word is copied into the story in progress. If they cannot find the word they are looking for on the list, I write the word on the lines provided in the Enterprise Speller. The student then copies it into her story. It is an opportunity for the child to learn the word she wants to learn, in standard form, as she copies the correct spelling of that word the teacher or adult volunteer has just written.

Spelling words correctly seems to help students demonstrate more confidence while writing a story. They learn to write fluently as they practice writing in most of their learning experiences. Writing is also a means to check for concept comprehension, as well as a platform for artistic and literary expression. An integrated curriculum, organized in units, provides students with enriching experiences where they naturally make connections. Student examples of integrated writing activities and other writing examples of student work demonstrate how quality tools are used with the assignments.

Writing in Science

Primary-age children think that science is very important. Their interest and focus are captured immediately when they engage in developmentally appropriate science activities. My yearly plan is divided into three extensive science units: insects (life science), solids and liquids (physical science), and air and weather (earth science). These topics are enriched by some shorter units.

Factual Writing About Insects

The life-science unit on insects is based on curriculum developed by *Full Option Science Systems (FOSS)*[6] (see Appendix B for more information). "One of Dr. Deming's admonitions was, 'Learn from the masters; they are few.'"[7] We continue to learn from the masters at Lawrence Hall of Science. Each time we study the curriculum I listen to my customers (students and parents) and make every attempt to implement their ideas and suggestions for improvement. "Never stop improving. Define improvement in every aspect of schooling (curriculum) and continually show progress" is the fifth of Dr. Deming's fourteen points, as rephrased for education.[8]

One class's suggestions for improvement influenced Dr. Larry Lowery, of Lawrence Hall of Science, to modify the design of a butterfly puzzle activity. Students modified a completed paper butterfly puzzle design by adding a popsicle stick for strength and a string so it could be pulled through the air like a kite. They were so excited by how well their ideas worked that I suggested they write a letter to Dr. Lowery. He quickly wrote a letter thanking them for the improvements they had made on the original design and mentioned he would be using their modification idea in future publications.

Figure 5.1 shows an integrated web of several academic subjects with a focus on insects. The following ideas are examples of some writing activities we do during the first eight weeks of school. We usually study one insect in depth per week, starting with butterflies. Live painted lady butterfly larvae are ordered from a biological laboratory to spend their entire life cycle in the classroom habitat. The butterfly larvae inspire the students to write. I purposely do not tell them what kind of larvae they are observing. Written scientific observations, as well as predictions of what the larvae will become, are examples of nonfictional or factual writing.

The children are also encouraged to bring in harmless insects from their yards. Bringing local insects into the classroom gives students the opportunity to draw from background knowledge and prior experiences with the insects. Children have insect stories to tell and, given the opportunity, will write them. I challenge students to extend their learning through use of expository texts in the classroom and school libraries, as well as the Internet, and to write a report about their insects.

The two events that follow provided some wonderful factual writing experiences for the students. During September 1997 a student brought in a praying mantis. It later made an egg case on the lid of the habitat. We watched and wondered in anticipation until May 1998, when at least thirty tiny baby praying mantis hatched out in the classroom. The children were very motivated to write about this event. On another occasion, a school employee found a monarch butterfly chrysalis and brought it into the classroom for the children to observe and make predictions about what kind of insect would come out. Two weeks later, while we were at lunch, it hatched out, and we walked back into the classroom to find a monarch butterfly hanging down from its chrysalis. I seized the moment, making quick changes in our normal afternoon schedule to allow the children to write a report about the event. Anticipating the event, I had precut orange butterflies using the Ellison Cutter™. (This die-cutting machine is a very useful and time-saving tool. Ordering information is included in Appendix B.) The students glued the cut-outs onto the report paper and added the distinctive black and white markings with crayons. As the butterfly's wings were drying I allowed the butterfly to crawl onto my hand, and then onto the students' hands. I took photographs of each student holding the butterfly. The photographs were later glued onto pieces of lined paper for a future writing lesson.

Once students have studied many butterflies and moths, a force field analysis would be an useful tool to use during a lesson in comparison (see chapter 3).

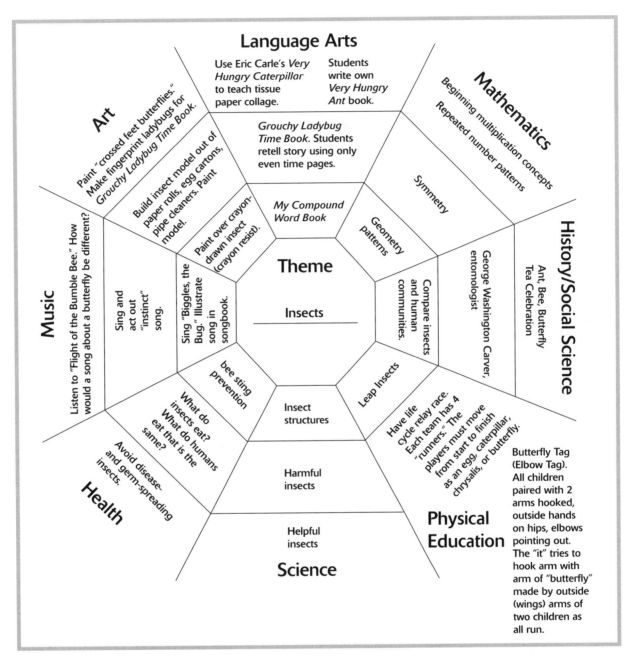

Figure 5.1. Unit web for insects.

Writing from Expository Text Experience

Rookie Read-About Science™ texts like *It's a Good Thing There Are Insects*, by Allan Fowler, provide large color photographs and a minimal amount of text that most primary children can read successfully. I also make small books to connect a writing experience with a reading experience.

Once the three body-part shapes and six attached legs are brought to their attention, many primary-grade students can look at an insect and draw a resemblance. However, drawing experiences with pencil or crayon can easily become mundane. Students who struggle to express themselves artistically sometimes just stare at a blank piece of paper, too discouraged to attempt an illustration, much less write a story. Students can be given a variety of creative experiences using several art mediums with planned follow-up writing assignments.

Variation of Art Experiences Provides a Catalyst for Writing

The artwork acts as a catalyst, igniting the thinking processes necessary to give a written response. Thus each piece of artwork becomes the illustration for the next writing assignment. The following are examples of some activities.

Students enjoy making models of insects with available paper-towel tubes, egg cartons, pipe cleaners, and other craft items in the classroom or at home as a homework project to be constructed with a family member. Upon completion of the insect models and the accompanying reports, they present their projects to the class. After hearing a presentation, other classmates are often motivated to construct an insect model and write a report. The models can be suspended from the ceiling with fishing line.

The Crossed Feet Butterflies[9] activity begins with each child standing on a piece of white art paper with his legs crossed at the ankles. Someone else traces around his shoes, because the student usually falls over if he tries to do the tracing. The art paper is folded in half from top to bottom. After the student lays the paper flat, a few drops of paint are spread on one side only. The unpainted side is laid over the top of the other, pressing them together. When the paper is opened, the student sees a beautiful symmetrical flip pattern. This activity can be extended naturally to a math lesson in symmetry and a writing assignment.

Math Manipulatives Can Stimulate Writing Ideas

Math manipulatives can be used successfully to inspire writing ideas. Pattern blocks and many other math manipulatives are used to "assist the writing process by becoming a 'user-friendly' vehicle for designing pictures. The pattern block art then becomes the catalyst for student writing"[10] (Figure 5.2).[11] (See Appendix E for more ideas on using math manipulatives to illustrate stories.)

In addition to many mathematical uses, Pattern Blocks assist the writing process by becoming a user-friendly vehicle for designing pictures. The pattern block art then becomes the catalyst for student writing.

Materials

- Pattern Blocks
- Pattern Block Template
- Pencil
- Drawing paper or ditto paper
- Writing paper (preferably without dotted lines and heavy enough to not tear when children erase)
- Crayons

Process

1. Child designs picture using pattern blocks.
2. Child gathers plain sheet of ditto or art paper, pattern block template, and pencil.
3. Child reproduces the pattern block picture on unlined paper.
4. Child colors pattern block picture and adds finishing touches.
5. Child attaches writing paper to picture and writes story.

Pattern Blocks

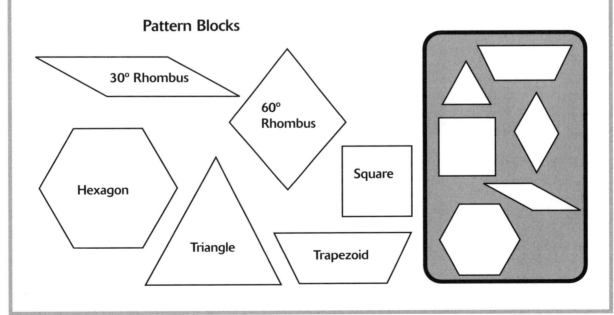

Figure 5.2a. Pattern block writing ideas. Designed by Sandra L. Jenkins, used with permission.

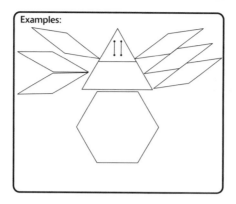

Adaptations:

1. Pattern Block designs may be reproduced with Pattern Blocks cut from construction paper using the Ellison Letter Cutter. When the geometric shapes are pasted on black construction paper the contrast is quite impresive.

2. The writing and art may both be completed on unlined paper. Heavy lined paper may be placed under the writing paper as a guide. Unlined paper, using the guide, gives children complete creative freedom in the placement of the language, in relationship to the art, without compromising quality and neatness.

3. Pattern Block designs can also be reproduced with Pattern Block sponge shapes and paint or with Pattern Block rubber stamps. Ellison Letter Company markets both sponge and rubber stamp materials that can be cut. To make rubber stamps, adhere the cut-out, self-adhesive, rubber stamp material to an actual Pattern Block and use a push pin for the handle of the stamp.

Figure 5.2b. Pattern block writing ideas. Designed by Sandra L. Jenkins, used with permission.

Children's Literature Inspires Writing from Children

Eric Carle's book *The Very Hungry Caterpillar* inspires my students to learn about collage. The text is typed, cut, and placed into a blank book. Torn tissue paper is used to illustrate each page. The story lends itself easily to retelling of the original storyline or rewriting of the original text. Students may choose any art medium to use for illustration.

After a choral reading of Eric Carle's *The Very Grouchy Ladybug,* the children write a retelling of the story, usually writing one page per day. The time is drawn on the clock face on each page. A collection of different art mediums are used to illustrate each page. The students explore art mediums in the following ways: by sketching with pencil; making fingerprint ladybugs by coloring the tip of a finger with red marker; creating teacher-guided drawing of the story's lobster and elephant; adding detail to the setting with colored markers; making a gorilla by the torn construction paper technique; using twisted tissue paper to make a boa constrictor wrapped around a construction-paper tree; and using crayon resist with a dye wash to create a unique cover. Each student can express her art uniquely while using the same art medium. Art, math (writing in the time on the analog clock face), reading, and writing are integrated in this project.

This project may be extended by using the Ellison Cutter™ to cut out two black construction-paper circles (one small and the other large) for the head and abdomen, one black trapezoid for the thorax, two half-circle red shells, and two wax-paper half-shells to represent wings. The students then glue their ladybug parts onto the paper and draw dots, six legs, and two antennae. Once the paper ladybug is completed, the students write their own ladybug stories. This idea turns a more structured writing activity into an open-ended assignment within the same theme. More insects can be constructed and other stories can be written. Student interest is a key factor.

An Integrated Science, Writing, Art, and Math Project

The Ants Go Marching One by One, a camp song, lends itself naturally to having students make up their own rhymes at the end of each phrase. Before students try their own rhymes, we brainstorm rhyming words to list under each number, as in Figure 5.3.

The students fill in the ending word of each phrase with the rhyme of their choice. They are given squared paper, which is easily cut down from the rectangular shape and stapled into a book. A phrase is written on each page. A math component is added to the songbook as an illustration. Students use base-ten unit cubes to build square numbers, page by page. For example, here is the procedure for building the number nine: the students make a three-by-three square with cubes (Figure 5.4).

Simple instructions are:

1. *Build it.* Make a three-by-three square out of base-ten unit cubes.

2. *Trace it.* Trace around the nine cubes.

3. *Cut it.* Cut out the square number.

4. *Glue it.* Glue it onto the page above the text in the square student-made songbook.

one	two	three	four
sun	shoe	tree	door
thumb	dew	me	shore
gun	glue	knee	core

Figure 5.3. Brainstorming rhyming words.

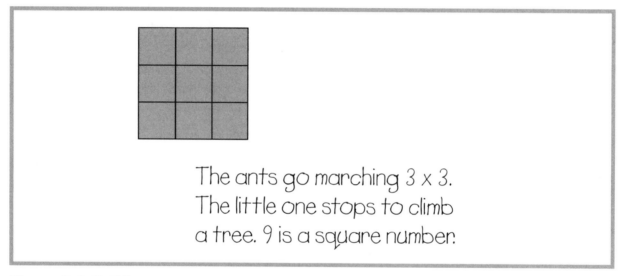

The ants go marching 3 x 3.
The little one stops to climb
a tree. 9 is a square number.

Figure 5.4. Building square numbers with "ants" and math manipulatives.

To make it easier for some students, you can use multi-link cubes and one-inch-grid paper instead of centimeter-grid paper. The cover of *My Square Number Book* is designed by using a straight edge to draw straight lines making square letters. In addition, the students can draw the same amount of insects on the page as the unit cubes, around the edge, evenly spaced like a border. Due to its open-ended nature, *The Square Number Book* can continue until the teacher brings closure, depending on student interest.

To extend this activity, have the children refer to their songbooks as they make up their own song by changing the insect, as in the following example:

"The grasshoppers go hopping one by one.
Hurrah! Hurrah!
The grasshoppers go hopping one by one.
Hurrah! Hurrah!
The grasshoppers go hopping one by one,
The little ones stop to eat a plum
And they all go hopping around and around
To get out of the rain.
Boom! Boom! Boom! Boom! Boom! Boom!"

Writing in Skill Booklets

Learning and practicing specific writing skills during a portion of their language arts time can help children become better at writing. Many writing conventions can be taught and practiced by using the format in the skill booklets.[12] The structure of the skill booklet and inside pages is such that the basic template can be adapted to meet the specific needs of students in any unit of study. Students are provided with a cover and several inside pages stapled together to form the booklet. On the top line the students write the word being studied, be it a noun, compound word, prefix, or so on. There is space in the middle for an illustration, and the bottom of the page has lines for writing the word in a sentence(s). The students and I decide how many pages to put in the booklets and the duration of the lesson. A typical skill booklet assignment can begin on Monday and be completed by Friday. Students may use a skill booklet to write and illustrate *My Book of Characters* from a second-grade core literature book, or to collect their wishes in *My Book of Wishes*. Another skill booklet project might be to gather adjectives that describe nouns in *My Book of Adjectives,* or to make a collection of compound words in *My Book of Compound Words*.

The next example demonstrates the versatility of the skill booklet. When my students make their own *My Book of Jokes and Riddles*, I flip several pages of the inside-page master upside down, fold the cover and inside pages together in half, staple the pages and cover them together. Flipping the master allows my students more room on which to write their jokes. (The joke, in the form of a question or riddle, needs more room than the answer.) Students illustrate the joke or riddle in the circle and write the answer on the single line. (An extensive list of skill-booklet-cover masters and inside-sheet masters is available in Appendix C. Some may be more suitable as extensions for primary students who need extra challenges.)

Writing in a Venn Diagram

The venn diagram is another format in which students can write compound words. The small words are placed in the outside part of the circles. The students make a compound word by connecting two small words from the outside part of the circles and write the compound word in the middle of the intersecting circles (Figure 5.5). The venn diagram format is useful when comparing characters from a story or insect structures.

The writing ideas and examples I have given so far in this chapter are only a few of the many possibilities that can be used. Opportunities for writing experiences are as numerous as the types of insects in the world. Teacher-supply stores have many shelves of books loaded with wonderful ideas written by adult authors trying to help teachers motivate children to write. Student interest seems to be a key factor.

Students in the primary grades want to write about their areas of interest, experiences, and friends. When their stories are valued and celebrated, they want to write more. Periodically we have unit-end celebrations when we invite the parents into our classroom. The class run chart is displayed, so all the parents can view our continuous improvement in learning life-science concepts. Why wait until Open House late in the spring to celebrate the student scientists and authors in our classroom? These celebrations are like the seventh-inning stretch during an exciting baseball game that may continue until the bottom of the eleventh inning. The students enjoy celebrating in the midst of their ongoing learning experiences, moving from one unit into the next. My students (customers) must *"maintain enthusiasm while increasing learning."*[13]

Other writing ideas, as well as uses of some quality tools, are incorporated into our solids and liquids science unit.

Writing about Solids and Liquids

The physical-science unit on solids and liquids is based on curriculum developed by *Full Option Science Systems (FOSS™)*.[14] Figure 5.6 displays integration of several academic subjects with a focus on solids and liquids. The following are samples of some of the writing activities.

Similes

The students participate in a bubble-art project during which they blow bubbles in a soap mixture colored with blue paint. A clean piece of paper is laid

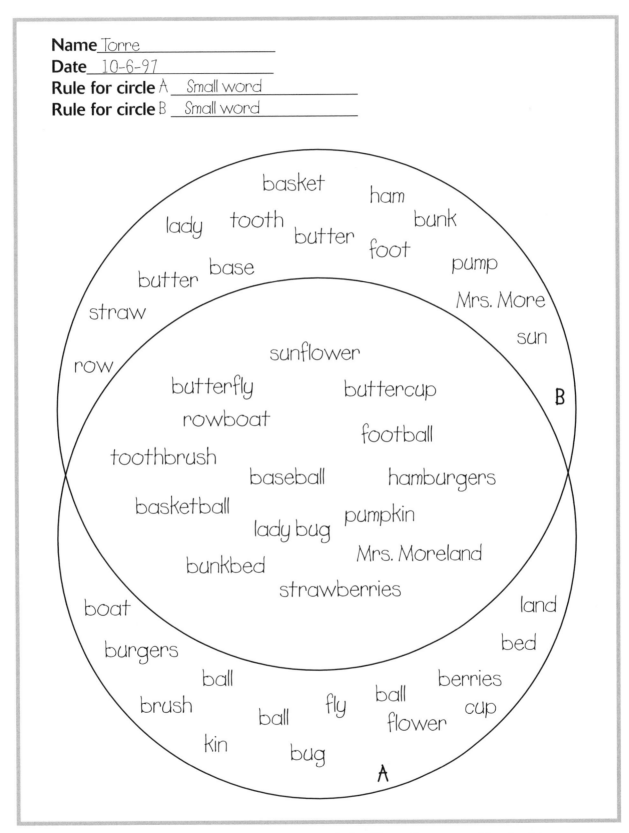

Name Torre
Date 10-6-97
Rule for circle A   Small word
Rule for circle B   Small word

basket
ham
lady   tooth   bunk
butter
butter   base   foot   pump
straw   Mrs. More
row   sun
sunflower
butterfly   buttercup
rowboat   football
toothbrush
baseball   hamburgers
basketball   pumpkin
lady bug
Mrs. Moreland
bunkbed
strawberries
boat   land
burgers   bed
ball   berries
brush   fly   ball   cup
ball   flower
kin   bug
B
A

Figure 5.5. Venn diagram for compound words by Torre Swanson. Used with permission.

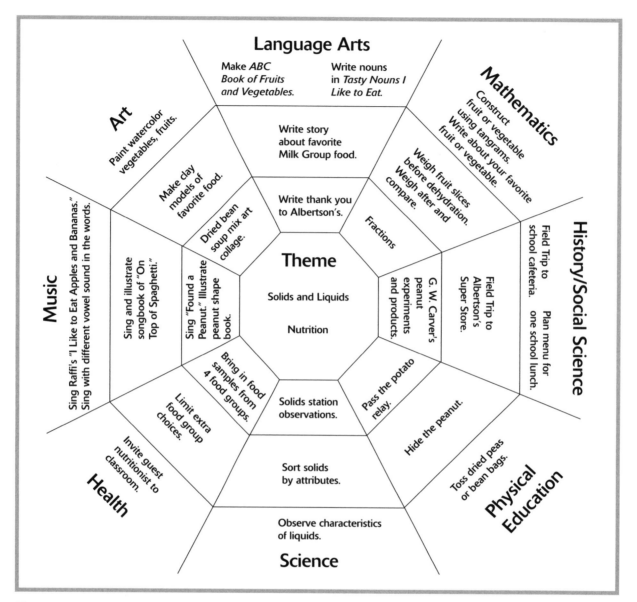

Figure 5.6. Unit web for solids and liquids.

onto the pile of bubbles. After it dries, the arrangement of bubbles is outlined and students write a simile describing the bubble art.

Affinity Diagram

Students pull mixed-up food-picture cards out of a box when beginning a new unit in nutrition. An affinity diagram is used to categorize the picture cards into the four food groups and the extra food group.

Field Trip Thank-You Letter Ideas

After a field trip to the school cafeteria, we make an art project using construction-paper scraps to represent the balanced snack the cooks made for us from the four food groups. We brainstorm ideas about the experience once we get back into class. The students construct paper containers by folding up all four sides of the paper and taping each corner so the sides stand up, representing a cafeteria tray. The paper "snack" is glued into the container. The snack is glued onto a thank-you letter. The students write about their favorite parts of the field trip and thank the cooks for the tour and snack. The cooks proudly display them by taping them up all around the cafeteria's serving window.

Writing about the field trip to the school kitchen is an example of how writing is inspired by an experience. After every field trip we follow the same process, using another creative art idea that symbolizes something unique to the experience. The students write thank-you notes or letters, make a book, or so on, to thank the local businesses we visit. The following are two examples:

1. When we visited a local supermarket, students went "shopping" for examples of the four food groups and organized them in the correct column. Upon our arrival back to school, each student wrote and illustrated about their favorite part of the supermarket tour. We compiled all of the stories, bound it, and gave it to the manager of the supermarket as a thank-you gift.

2. After returning from a field trip at a local hospital, the students wrote thank-you letters on one side of large Band-Aid™-shaped pieces of white paper. The students decorated the other side like children's Band-Aids™. The sheets are then bound, made into a book, and given to the hospital guide volunteers.

Students Illustrate Their Own Alphabet

The classroom alphabet, which is located above the white boards, is always illustrated by the students. The goal is to change the illustrations after every unit. There's no need to purchase the classroom alphabet. The children write a sentence that describes their illustration. This is a wonderful way to review past learning, and students enjoy this open-ended activity. I offer different art mediums or math manipulatives each time the alphabet is illustrated. After the project is taken down from the alphabet area on the wall, it is made into a plastic spiral-bound book called *The ABC Book of*

Fruits and Vegetables and placed in our classroom library to be enjoyed during self-selected reading time.

Spatial relations are captured by the mind when the hands slide, rotate, and flip objects. Pattern blocks require students to slide and rotate, but tangrams require additionally that students flip the pieces. Consequently, tangrams are more difficult and more powerful for students than many other math manipulatives.[15] (See Figure 5.7.)

Priority Matrix

Every year, the school's head cook confidently allows our second-grade class to assemble a meal based on the four food groups because she believes we are nutrition experts. Our suggestion is placed on the school's menu for the following month and submitted to the head cook's boss at the district office for final approval. It is approved every year.

We begin the process by looking over the previous month's lunch menu. The children fill out a priority matrix, a quality tool, rating the main-dish choices from the meat group from first choice to eighth choice (Figure 5.8). (A priority matrix master can be found in Appendix A). After reviewing the data, pizza is found to be their favorite choice. Then a survey is provided to choose the rest of the balanced-meal choices and the choices are graphed. The children are thrilled to have this opportunity to choose the balanced-lunch meal for six hundred other children at our school for one day of the year.

Writing in Math

"If we consistently analyze what we do and adjust to get better, we will improve!"[16] "I believe that specific goals are the most vital ingredient of purpose. Improvement cannot occur without them."[17] At the beginning of the new school year I set a specific goal to adjust my instructional strategies to help individual students improve their understanding of math concepts. I am determined to gather weekly data from random assessments of math concepts, in order to study and make necessary changes to help my students improve their understanding of a confusing concept.

Materials

- Sets of Tangrams
- Collection of Tangram pictures
- Tangram template
- Pencil
- Drawing or ditto paper
- Writing paper
- Crayons

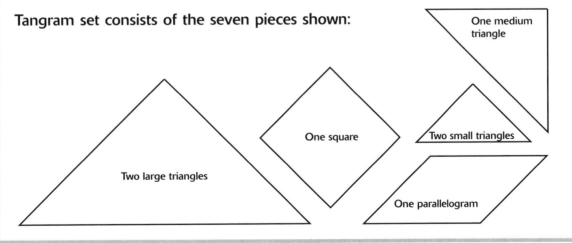

turtle

Process

1. Child selects tangram picture.

2. Child takes set of tangrams and places on tangram picture. All seven pieces fit into shape exactly.

3. Child gets plain ditto paper, tangram template and pencil.

4. Child reproduces tangram picture onto blank ditto paper using the tangram template to show where each of the seven pieces fits in the design.

5. Child adds detail to tangram picture; completes any desired finishing touches.

6. Child writes story to accompany tangram illustration.

Tangram set consists of the seven pieces shown:

One medium triangle

One square

Two small triangles

Two large triangles

One parallelogram

Figure 5.7. Writing ideas with tangrams. (Designed by Sandra L. Jenkins, used with permission.)

Continuous Improvement in the Primary Classroom

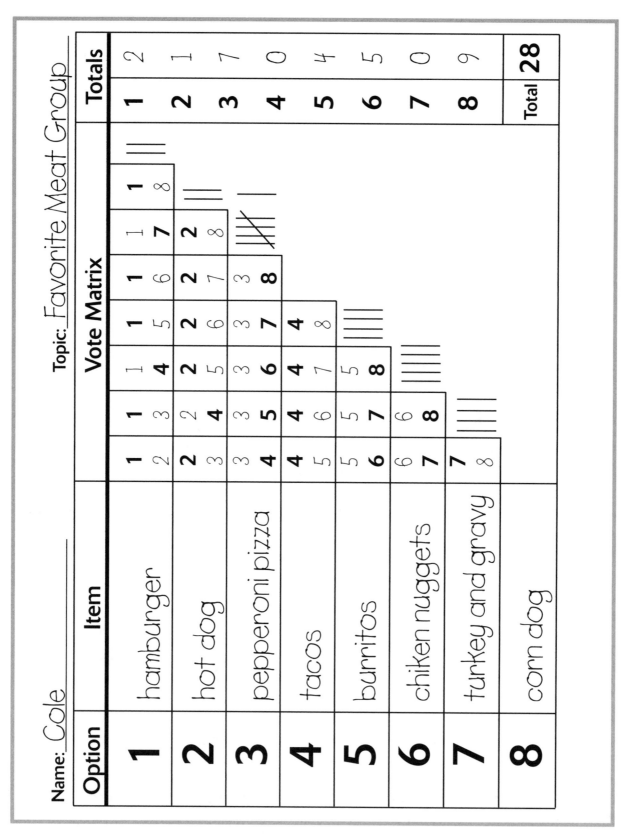

Name: Cole   Topic: Favorite Meat Group

Figure 5.8. Student example of priority matrix by Cole Geiger. Used with permission.

The vehicle that drives the instruction is an assessment tool called *Enterprise Weekly and Problem Solving*™.[18] The thoroughly researched second-grade (other binders are compiled for first through eighth grade) binder ensures each week's random (preview/review) problems will

---

. . . focus on the Enterprise Math Concepts students should know by the end of grade 2. The first problem each week is a review of the Kindergarten math concepts (#1–10). The second problem each week is a review of the first grade math concepts (#11–10). The third and fourth problems each week are material new to second grade (#21–40). The fifth problem each week is a random problem from #1–40.[19]

The weekly assessment is organized into a spiral-bound lined notebook called *My Very Own Math Journal*. The math journal idea came from another master teacher, Peggy McLean, during a weeklong math workshop in 1996. It is structured so that the teacher can "make the activity safe and successful for everyone,"[20] because the difficulty of the math concept can be raised or lowered, depending on the child's level of understanding. Asking a child to write how she solved the math problem is like adding icing to a cake. It enhances the understanding of the math problem. When the child isn't required to explain her thinking by writing it down, the teacher can only guess how the child arrived at the answer.

Every Monday morning we follow the same procedure: The Enterprise Weekly™ is glued onto the left side of the notebook. The right side of the notebook is left blank, and is available for extra practice or extension of any of the five concepts the next day. Later in the day, I record the number correct on each student's first attempt into the Class Action™ spreadsheet and print a class run chart. The process data are used to inform instruction. The next day's (sometimes the next several days') lesson is prepared for each child by writing more problems on the right side of the spiral notebook page. Math manipulatives are used to help the child visualize the concept. The goal is to create a follow-up lesson where the child can explain how he figured out the answer.

Math journals have been part of my math program for two years. I am convinced the students demonstrate understanding of math concepts when they draw an illustration representing the mathematical ideas, write a math equation that clarifies the illustration, and explain in writing how they understand the concept represented by the answer.

Data are gathered each Monday from an assessment of random (preview/review) math concepts. This is identical to the procedure used for spelling in chapter 4. A class run chart is displayed weekly in the classroom. Student run charts overlaid onto a class scatter diagram communicate progress to parents. The data inform my math instruction throughout the rest of the week. Math concepts are revisited and practiced in other problem-solving challenges.

Flowchart

A flowchart is a quality tool that sequences the most important steps in a process. It can be also used to illustrate morning routine procedures, how to check out a library book, how to solve a subtraction problem, and so on. The students and I make a flowchart to help us follow the correct steps when attempting a problem-solving challenge. (See Figure 5.9; a master copy can be found in Appendix D.)

Writing a Dichotomous Key and Error Guide

There are areas in my writing program where I need to improve my classroom system. In the future, I plan to start collecting data using a dichotomous key to help my students improve their skills and fluency in writing. A colleague helped me modify (for second grade) the dichotomous key he designed for eighth-grade writing assignments. Graphing common errors from the error guide will help to pinpoint my instruction (Figure 5.10). Another area where I haven't collected data is in math problem solving. My classroom system will continue to improve as I gather new data to inform my instruction.

In summary, Chapter 5 shows how to provide meaningful instruction and assignments, while writing across the curriculum and focusing on the aim: "Maintain enthusiasm while increasing learning."[21] Students improve their understanding of concepts through written responses, thus demonstrating the transfer of information into knowledge. Researchers claim that

> Because writing processes are closely tied to cognitive processes, a natural link exists between writing and thinking. Writing across the curriculum for the purpose of strengthening learning carries the assumption that, somehow, the processes of writing will lead to better understandings of ideas and concepts, many of which students encounter in their readings across content areas.[22]

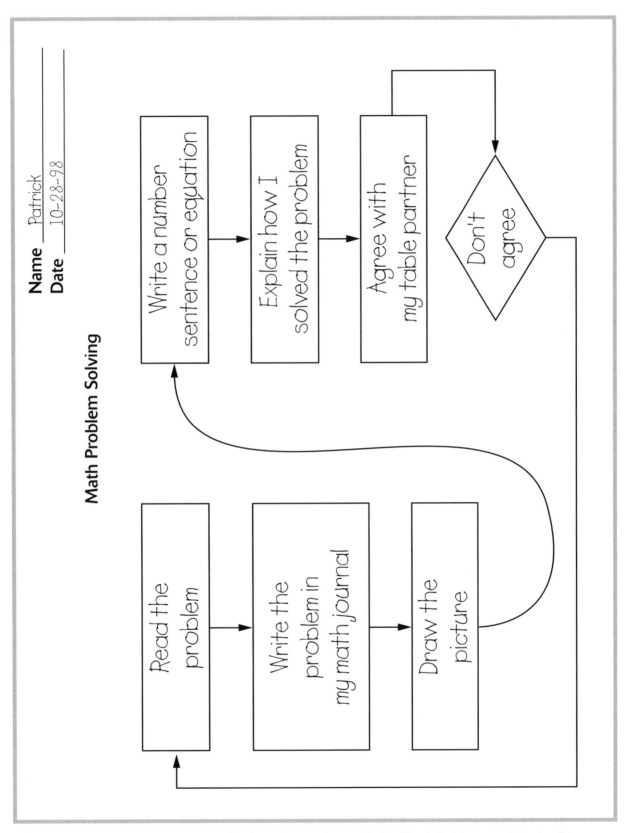

Figure 5.9. Student example of a flowchart. Artwork by Patrick Howser. Used with permission.

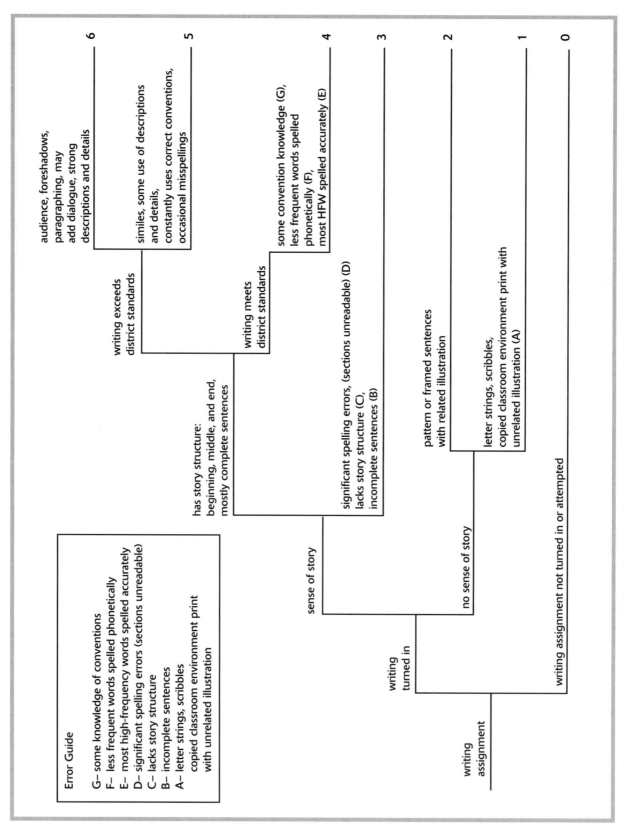

Figure 5.10. Dichotomous key with error guide for writing assessment.

Through daily writing lessons and experiences, second-grade students will be better prepared as fluent writers for their third-grade teachers and beyond.

In chapter 6, continuous improvement processes are used for many reading assessments and classroom instruction strategies.

Notes

1. Karin Dahl and Nancy Farnan, *Children's Writing: Perspectives from Research* (Newark, DE: International Reading Association, 1998), 62.
2. Lee Jenkins, *Improving Student Learning* (Milwaukee, WI: ASQ Quality Press, 1997), 115.
3. Gladys Rosencrans, *The Spelling Book* (Newark, DE: International Reading Association, 1998), 19.
4. Jenkins, *Improving Student Learning*, 25.
5. Rebecca Sitton, *Spelling Sourcebook* (Seattle, WA: Egger Publishing).
6. *Full Options Science Systems*, Lawrence Hall of Science, UC Berkeley. Chicago, IL: Encyclopedia Britannica Educational Corp., 1993. Insects.
7. Dahl and Farnan, *Children's Writing*, xix.
8. Ibid., 221.
9. Sharon Wheeler, *Butterflies and Moths* (Cypress, CA: Creative Teaching Press, 1990), 28.
10. Sandra Jenkins, "Implementing a Literature-Based Language Arts Program for Primary Grades" (thesis, Simpson College, n.d.), 36.
11. Ibid., 36–37.
12. Lee Jenkins, Whole Language Worksheet Masters, Enterprise School District teacher inservice, 1990.
13. Dahl and Farnan, *Children's Writing*, 115.
14. *Full Option Science Systems*, Lawrence Hall of Science, UC Berkeley, Chicago, IL: Encyclopedia Britannica Educational Corp., 1993. Solids and Liquids.
15. Jenkins, "Implementing a Literature-Based Language Arts Program for Primary Grades" (thesis, Simpson College, n.d.), 37.
16. Michael Schmoker, *Results: The Key to Continuous School Improvement* (Alexandria, VA: ASCD, 1996), 49.
17. Ibid., 23.
18. Judy Flores, Enterprise Weekly and Problem Solving, Enterprise School District, 1997.
19. Judy Flores, Memo to 2nd-grade teachers, Enterprise School District, Aug. 21, 1997.
20. Peggy McLean, Math Workshop at Enterprise District Office, July 29–Aug. 4, 1996.
21. Jenkins, *Improving Student Learning*, 115.
22. Dahl and Farnan, *Children's Writing*, 71.

CHAPTER 6

Reading Goals and Expectations

"Children are young, but they're not naive. And they're honest. They're not going to keep awake if the story is boring. When they get excited you can see it in their eyes."

CHINUA ACHEBE[1]

The purpose of chapter 6 is to explain how the students use a common class goal and constancy of purpose as they work together to read Accelerated Readers.™ I will also describe how I use process data in monthly reading assessments, to help me better meet the needs of individual students to improve their reading fluency. The graphs are included. An example lesson that integrates reading, math, and writing demonstrates the type of assignment that will "maintain enthusiasm while increasing learning."[2]

During a trimester conference a parent said to me, "What have you done to my daughter? All she wants to do is read after she gets home from school. In the past I have had to just about threaten her to get her to read with me! My parents [the student's grandparents] can't believe the change in her attitude toward reading." I showed the monthly reading-speed checks and other reading assessments I gave her daughter. Then I explained the process data on her line graph, which demonstrated continuous improvement in reading speed. I also told her about a class goal the children made during the second week of school to read 374 books before the winter break. Her daughter was enthused and contributing toward our classroom reading goal.

Classroom Reading Goals

In order to reach the classroom goal, each student is given the opportunity to read many books at his own instructional reading level. (See the section in chapter 1 entitled Accelerated Reader.™) Each student has to pass a computer-generated comprehension test designed for each book. After passing the test, the student fills in one of the little rectangles on a chart provided by a local pizza parlor. (The students and I figured out together that there were 374 rectangles on the chart.) The following describes how we set the goal.

When we first set our reading goal, I tried to lower the total amount before we all agreed and signed our names. As a part of the team, I wanted the children to have enough time to reach the lofty goal. But the children didn't want a smaller amount of books or an extension on the date. When they achieved their goal of 374 books two weeks *before* December 1st, I called the pizza parlor and asked if they would like to help us celebrate this achievement. They were astounded at the students' collective success. They donated three pizzas to help us celebrate the joy of reading.

The children were not working for an extrinsic reward, because I purposely did not mention this when they set their goal. However, it became part of the celebration after achieving their classroom goal. Each child's effort was an important part of the accomplishment of the total class goal. He or she was not in competition with another student. Every student made some progress in his or her reading fluency and comprehension. The joy of reading was the intrinsic reward for each child. By the end of the school year, our classroom of enthused readers set and achieved another reading goal.

The purpose for monthly reading-fluency checks is to document continuous improvement in every one of my students. The rationale behind the collection of process data in reading fluency is explained in the following excerpt:

Based upon the research of Dr. Mark Shinn of University of Oregon, some teachers have been recording weekly their students' reading speed. The stop watch begins when the student reads the first word and stops one minute later. When students come to a word they don't know, the teacher provides the word. The total number of words read correctly, minus the words provided by the teacher, are tabulated and recorded on the run chart. . . . No psychological instrument is so sensitive to growth as the simple checking of reading speed each week.[3]

Each month I check my students' fluency in a passage I pick that is more difficult than their instructional reading level. Many students are reading less than 80 words per minute. Some of them struggle to get through the passage. That passage of text becomes a goal for them to reach. By the end of the year most children surpass that goal and are reading a more difficult text passage.

When I begin the reading-fluency check (I give the student a clean copy of the text), I mark the same story page every time I assess the student's reading fluency. A different colored pencil is used each month as the student reads for one minute. I note the miscues and analyze the data. After the student retells the story (from the beginning up to the point when time ran out), I ask further comprehension questions and ask the student to make a prediction about what will happen in the story when it is revisited the next month. The student's score is then recorded and graphed. After a couple of months, I expect to see some improvement in reading speed. If the child practices reading with a family member every night, and if the tests he reads in class are at his instructional reading level, fluency should be increasing. While watching the data monthly, I adjust my teaching strategies to accommodate the reader's needs through further, more in-depth reading assessments and follow-up activities. The confusions must be cleared up as soon as possible, in order to free the child to have some satisfaction and continued success with reading.

Student Comparison of Reading and Spelling Progress

One child was not a fluent reader when he arrived in my class. After monthly fluency checks, he became a fluent second-grade reader. His parents noted a difference in his self-image and attitude. His growth in learning to spell high-frequency words made continuous progress as well.

After studying the data on Figure 6.1, I noticed his gradual improvement in spelling almost paralleled his growth in reading. However, in week 12, there was a significant drop in the number of words he spelled correctly on the random weekly test. This drop was due to a special cause. His mother and I figured out that he had spent more time working on getting his first loose tooth out than on the spelling assessment. (Losing baby teeth in class can take precedence over anything else in progress.)

The weekly data can also show when a child is in distress due to circumstances outside of the classroom. The data often confirm a problem the teacher senses in a child. I can observe a child's performance in spelling and math concepts dip during exactly the same weeks that he feels acute stress due to circumstances beyond his control. Often the information I gather from the process data helps me plan other special interventions for the student. I modify my instructional practices to try to meet his needs, and request support from other staff members on his behalf. As Mike Schmoker wisely stated,

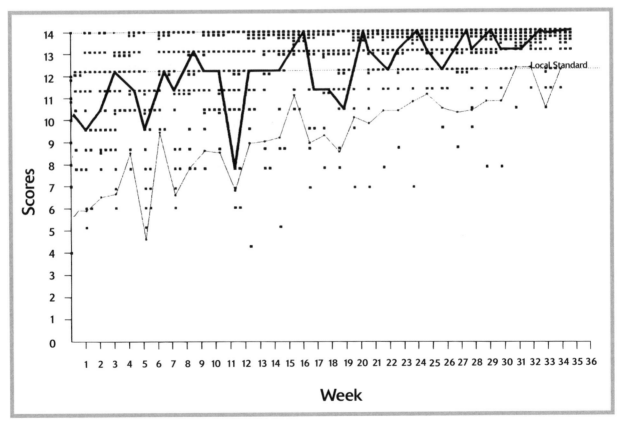

Figure 6.1. Class scatter matrix for spelling scores with student overlay.

"Data help monitor and assess performance. Just as goals are an essential element of success, so data are an essential piece of working toward goals. As with goals, data must be used judiciously and with discretion."[4]

Integrated Reading Comprehension, Writing, Art, and Math Lesson

The next activity is an example of the type of assignment my students enjoy, and which helps to "maintain enthusiasm while increasing learning"[5] in my classroom. It is an integrated reading comprehension, writing, art, and math lesson I developed from a book, *Three Pigs, One Wolf, and Seven Magic Shapes*, written by Grace Maccarone. After reading the text with their reading partners in the classroom, the students and I discuss how this version of *The Three Little Pigs* differs from the original story. The students use context clues and sequencing skills to find all the incomplete words. Once the character is known, all seven tangram pieces must be used to re-create each animal in the story line.[6] This activity helps the children with reading skills, writing, spatial relationships, rotating and displacement of geometric tangram pieces, and art. The students must write new, clever endings. Books like *Three Pigs, One Wolf, and Seven Magic Shapes* lend themselves to retelling, innovations and making inferences, including many natural math connections (see Appendix E).

Creating fun yet challenging comprehension activities for students helps them to connect with the storyline. Once a project is completed, the child has a sense of satisfaction and takes pride in her successful efforts. It reinforces a child's intrinsic motivation. There is joy in the eyes and on the face of a fluent reader.

In summary, every teacher wants his or her students to do well. Collecting data in reading fluency enables me to know exactly how my children are progressing each month. Process and results data will visibly affirm and validate the teacher's positive contributions toward students' academic development.

Notes

1. Chinua Achebe, *Teacher, A Little Book of Appreciation* (Philadelphia, PA: Running Press Book Publishers, 1999), 75.
2. Lee Jenkins, *Improving Student Learning* (Milwaukee, WI: ASQ Quality Press, 1997), 115.

3. Lee Jenkins, *Applying Quality Principles in Schools* (Cedar Rapids, IA: AASA Total Quality Network, 1995), 19.

4. Michael Schmoker, *Results: The Key to Continuous School Improvement* (Alexandria, VA, 1996), 29.

5. Jenkins, *Improving Student Learning*, 115.

6. The tangram is a puzzle that originated in China. It is a square cut into seven pieces: two large triangles, two small triangles, one medium triangle, one small square, and one parallelogram. The challenge is to put all seven pieces back together to make the original square shape. All seven pieces can also be used to re-create animals, characters from a story, design shapes, and so on.

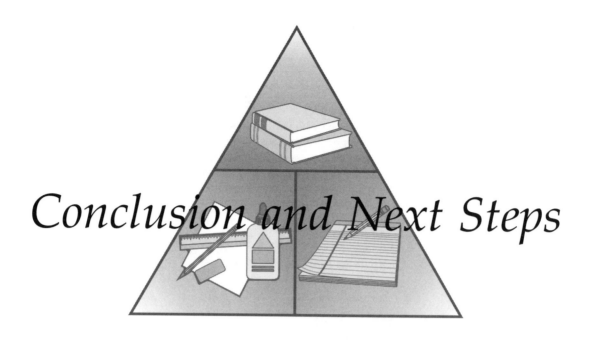

Conclusion and Next Steps

In conclusion, "Quality means getting to the bottom of a problem so it can be removed." "Today many countries around the world are putting Dr. Deming's ideas to work in factories, hospitals, and other businesses." "Dr. Deming believed team work, planning, and continuous improvement is the key to future success."[1] Students in many schools around the world are learning more by using his ideas.

There are many good educational vehicles available to teachers today. But when you use them, how do you know you are being effective? Data gathering is the missing piece. It helps you know if your instruction is effective or not. When I first started graphing data, I began with spelling, the subject in which I was most secure. I knew I could give a random test of fourteen high-frequency words each week. After I entered the number of words spelled correctly each week, the software program did all the work. I have been using a new software program for two years. I will continue to learn how to improve my spelling instruction using data collection and quality tools.

Teachers bear the burden of teaching all the required curriculum in a day. They have to make hundreds of decisions that affect their students' lives. Taking on one more task may seem overwhelming to you. It is my hope that you, the reader, will be encouraged by hearing about student successes. Start using the quality tools and data to drive the instruction so students will improve their performance on the journey of lifelong learning. With data, teachers can know on any week or any month during the year how well students in the classroom are performing. The students also want to help the teacher improve the classroom system. They usually know what they need. Together, teachers and students working as a team can improve their classroom system.

I am a common teacher producing uncommon results with quality tools. I succeed by helping others become successful. My challenge is that you begin gathering data so that you may feel the exhilaration of victory . . . watching your students perform well. You can use the data to make a difference in a struggling child, to monitor his learning and to find ways to help that student become successful in your classroom system. All students can succeed because data will show you when to adjust the course of your instruction, enabling *all* your students to learn the concepts you are trying so hard to teach! "Continuous improvement is nothing but the development of ever better methods."[2]

My true intent in writing this book is to encourage you in your own quality journey. If this has happened, it has been worth every second it took to write it. Thanks for taking time to read it. Truly, it's a gift from the heart of one dedicated teacher (and student of quality) to another. I conclude with some advice from Henry Ford: "Anyone who stops learning is old, whether at twenty or eighty. Anyone who keeps learning stays young. The greatest thing in life is to keep your mind young."[3]

Notes

1. Margaret Bynes, *Dr. Deming and His Amazing Quality Idea!* (Portales, NM: ProQue, 1997), 25–27.
2. Helio Gomes, *Quality Quotes* (Milwaukee, WI: ASQ Quality Press, 1996), 189.
3. Ibid., 122.

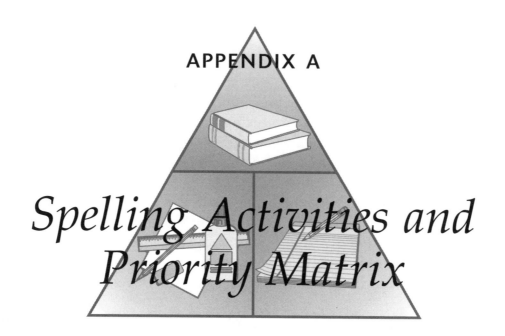

APPENDIX A

Spelling Activities and Priority Matrix

This appendix contains more examples of thematic spelling sentences, questions, songs, and poems written by Karen Fauss, or compiled from core literature and studied daily for at least a week to teach high-frequency words in context. Focus words are underlined, and are taken from Rebecca Sitton's list of high-frequency words.

Spelling question:

What are the names of the two very important men who were both born in the month of February?

PHONICS

Name: _____

Date: _____

| UPPERCASE | Lowercase | UPPERCASE |

_____
(word)

(picture)

_____
(word)

(picture)

_____
(word)

(picture)

Figure A.1. Phonics activity page.

Name _____   Date _____

High Utility Phonograms

My favorite words with this pattern are:

1. _____

2. _____

3. _____

Figure A.2. Phonogram activity page.

PHONICS

Write 12 words with double letters.

_____	_____
_____	_____
_____	_____
_____	_____
_____	_____
_____	_____

Graph

Double Vowels	Double Consonants		Double letters in same syllable	Double letters in different syllables

Figure A.3. Double-letter activity page.

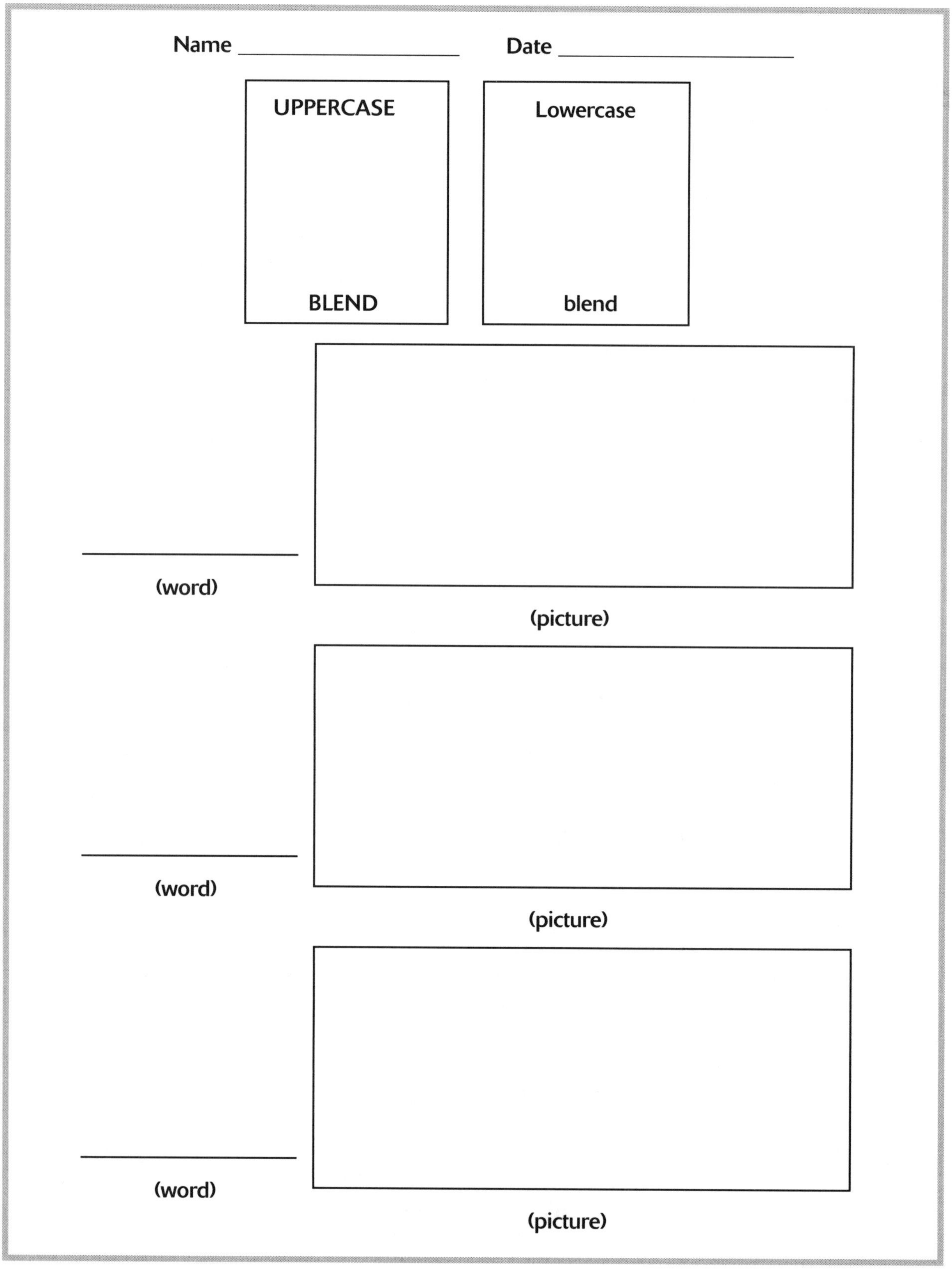

Name _____ Date _____

UPPERCASE	Lowercase
BLEND	blend

_____
(word)

(picture)

_____
(word)

(picture)

_____
(word)

(picture)

Figure A.4. Uppercase/lowercase activity page.

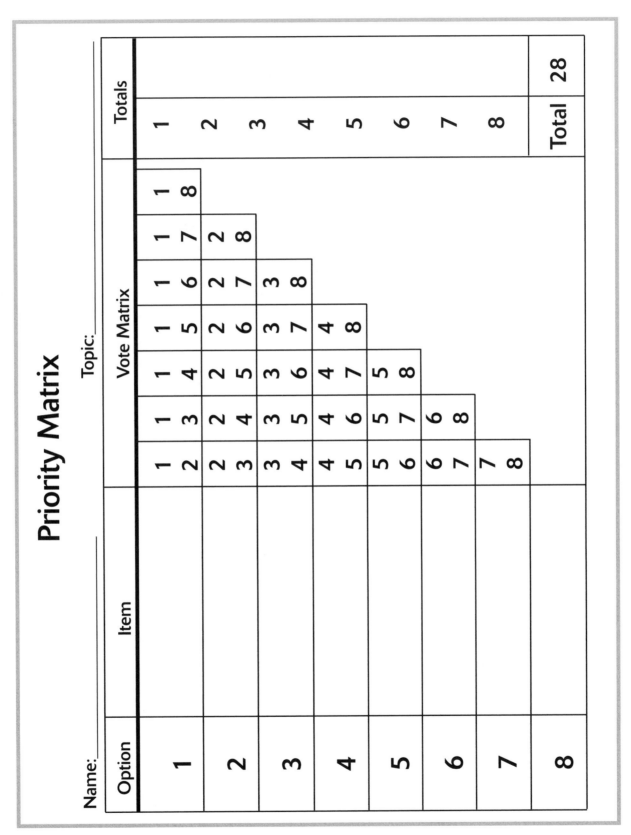

Figure A.5. Master priority matrix.

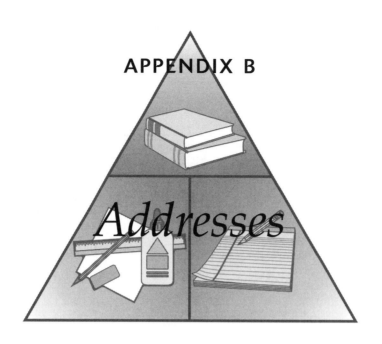

APPENDIX B

Addresses

Accelerated Reader™
Advantage Learning Systems
P.O. Box 8036
Wisconsin Rapids, WI 54495-8036

ASQ
P.O. Box 3066
Milwaukee, WI 53201-3060
www.asq.org or qualitypress.asq.org
Phone: 1-800-248-1946
Fax: 414-272-1734

Class Action™ **Software for Windows**
Developed by Blackthorne Publishing Company
Purchase from ASQ Quality Press, item #SW1064

Ellison Cutter ordering information:
Ellison Educational Equipment, Inc.
P.O. Box 8209
Newport Beach, CA 92658-8209
U.S.A. (800) 253-2238

Encyclopedia Britannica Educational Corporation 1993
310 South Michigan Avenue
Chicago, Illinois 60604
Insects, Solids and Liquids, Air and Weather
(Kits and Resource Binders)

Full Option Science Systems (FOSS)
1992 Regents, University of California
Lawrence Hall of Science
Berkeley, CA 94720

APPENDIX C

Skills Booklet Covers

A̲ll covers are designed by Lee Jenkins and used with permission.

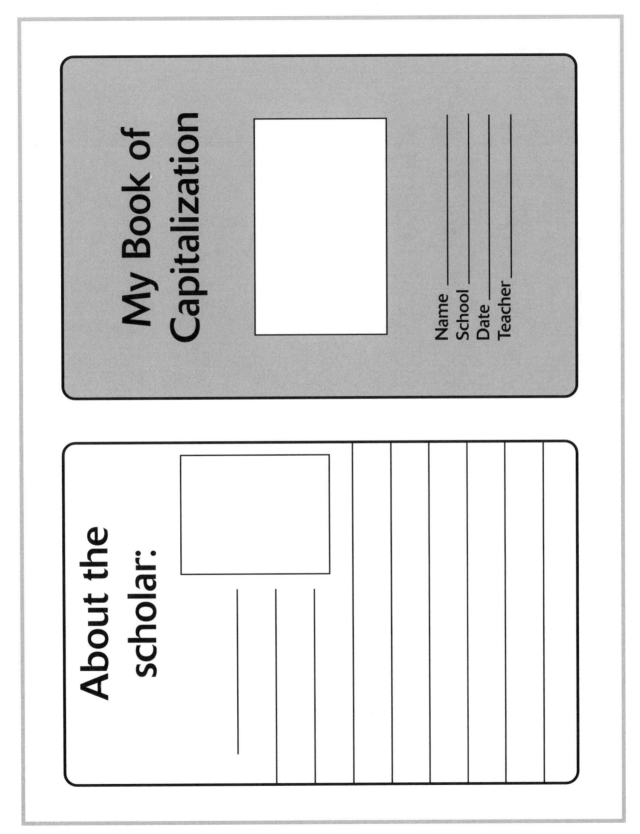

Figure C.1. *My Book of Capitalization.*

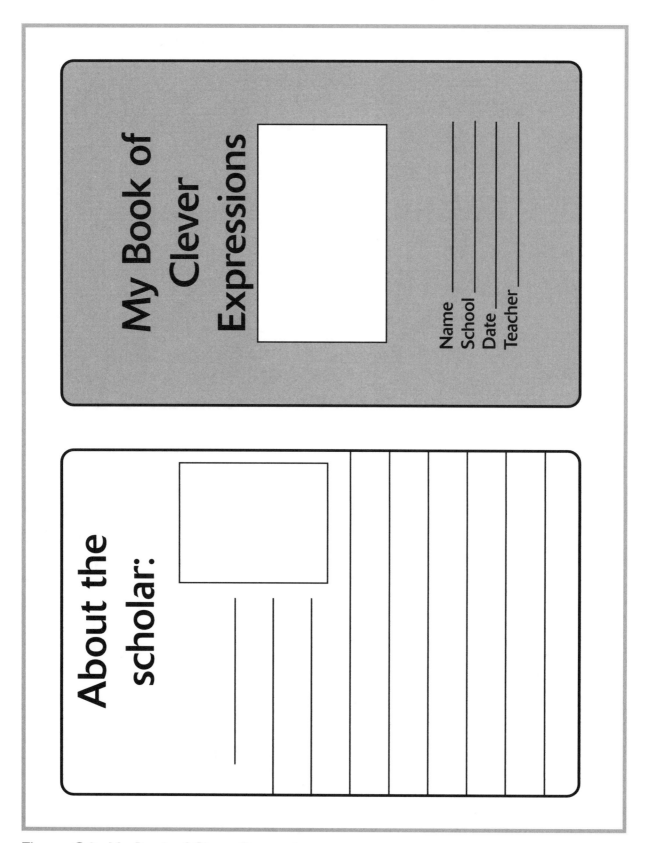

Figure C.2. *My Book of Clever Expressions.*

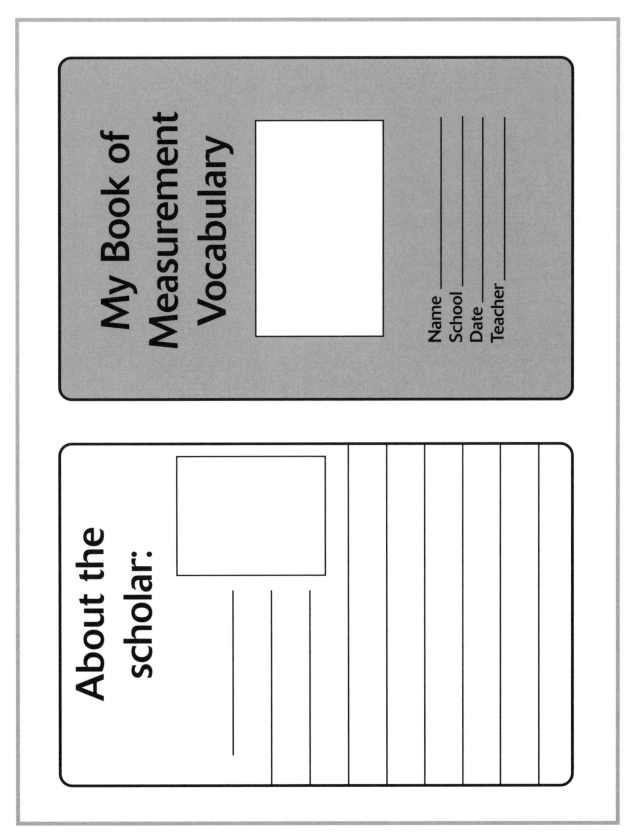

Figure C.3. *My Book of Measurement Vocabulary.*

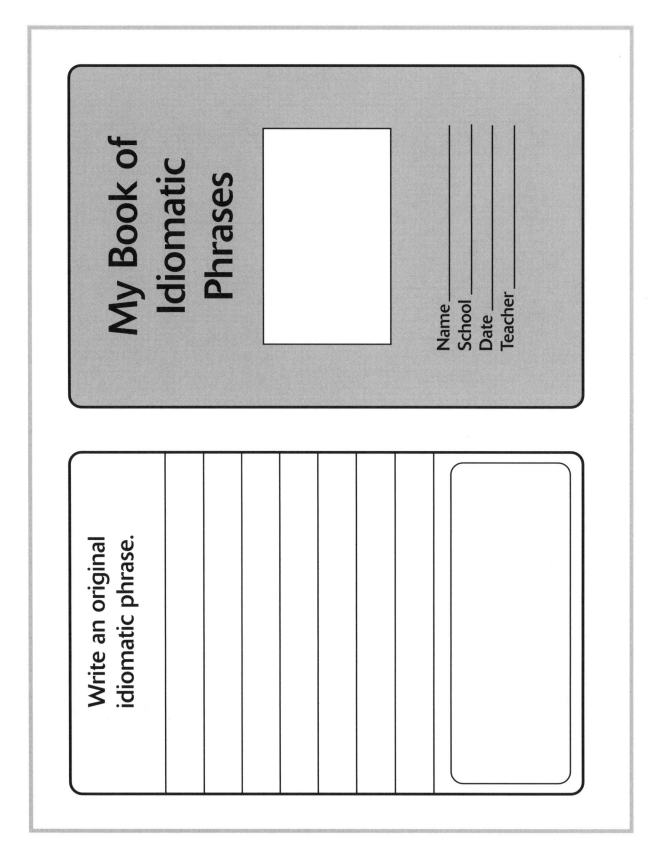

Figure C.4. *My Book of Idiomatic Phrases.*

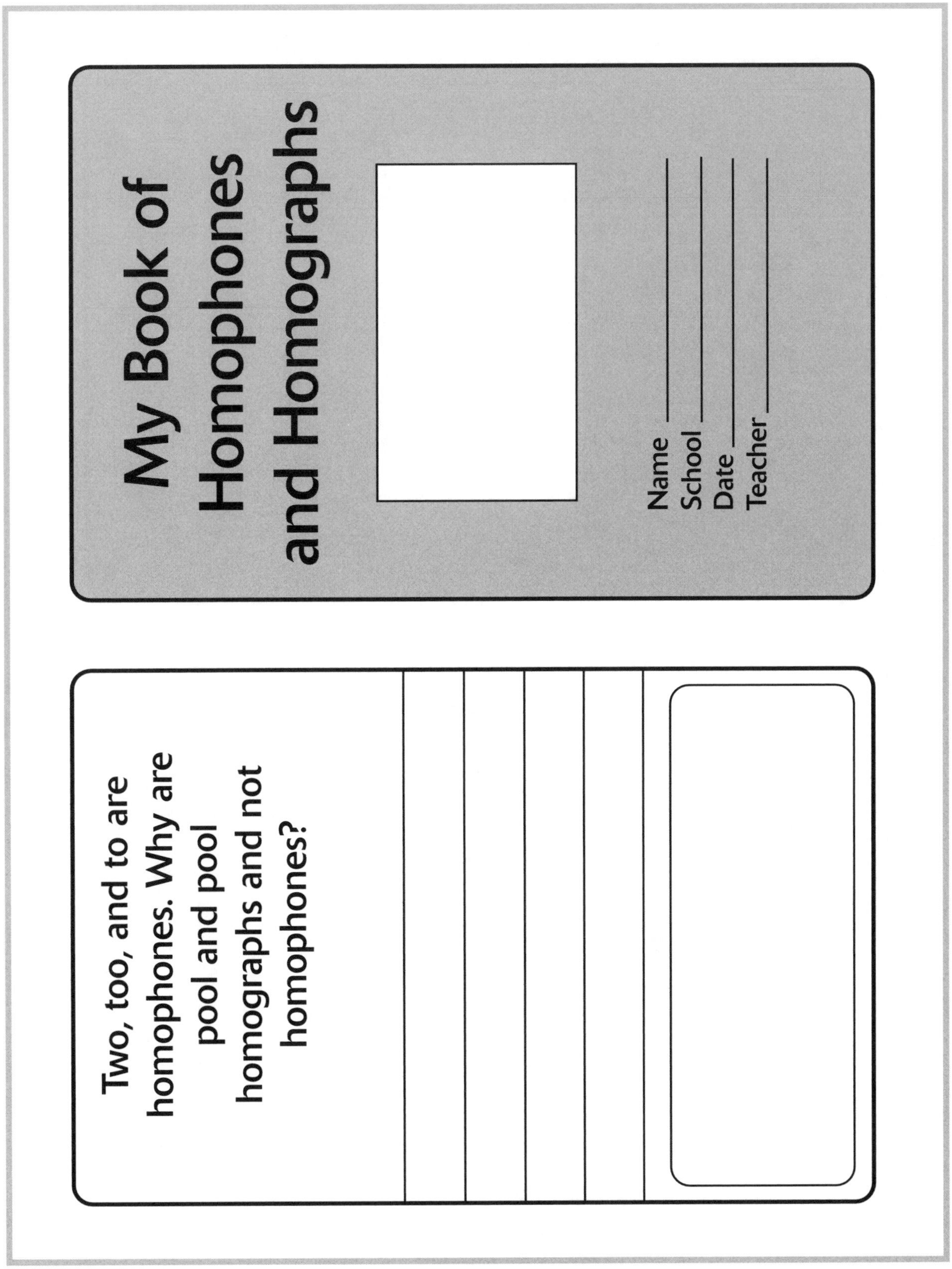

My Book of Homophones and Homographs

Name _____
School _____
Date _____
Teacher _____

Two, too, and to are homophones. Why are pool and pool homographs and not homophones?

Figure C.5. *My Book of Homophones and Homographs.*

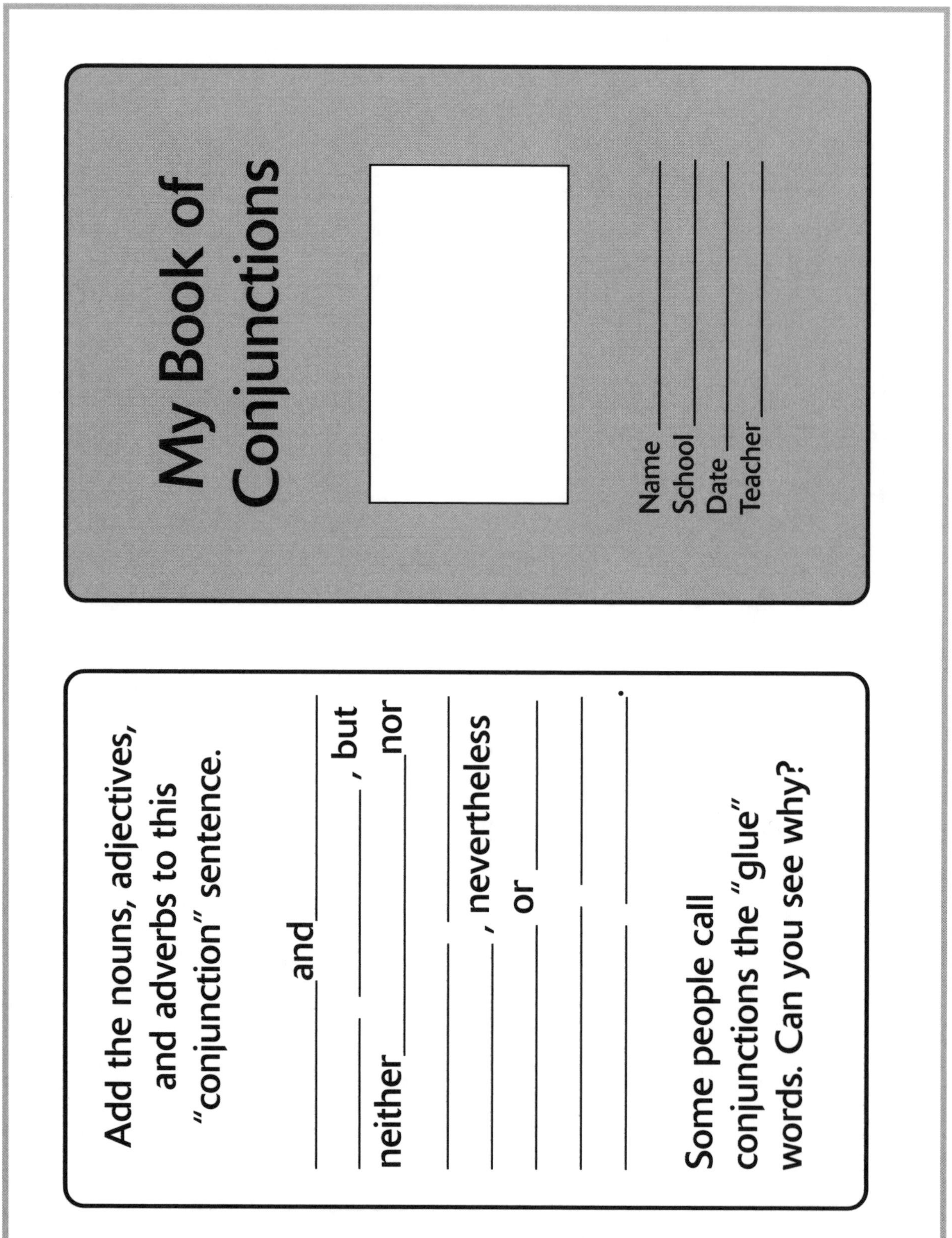

My Book of Conjunctions

Name _____
School _____
Date _____
Teacher _____

Add the nouns, adjectives, and adverbs to this "conjunction" sentence.

_____ and _____, but _____ nor

neither _____, nevertheless _____ or _____ .

Some people call conjunctions the "glue" words. Can you see why?

Figure C.6. *My Book of Conjunctions.*

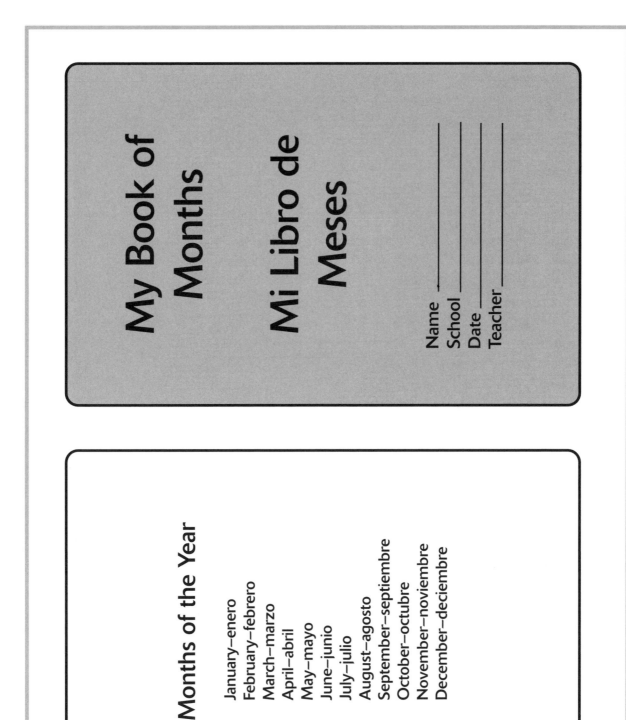

My Book of Months

Mi Libro de Meses

Name _____
School _____
Date _____
Teacher _____

Months of the Year

January–enero
February–febrero
March–marzo
April–abril
May–mayo
June–junio
July–julio
August–agosto
September–septiembre
October–octubre
November–noviembre
December–deciembre

Figure C.7. *My Book of Months.*

My Book of Adverbs

Name _____
School _____
Date _____
Teacher _____

These three adjectives below can be changed to adverbs by adding "ly."

1. _____
2. _____
3. _____

These three adjectives cannot be changed to adverbs by adding "ly."

1. _____
2. _____
3. _____

Figure C.8. *My Book of Adverbs.*

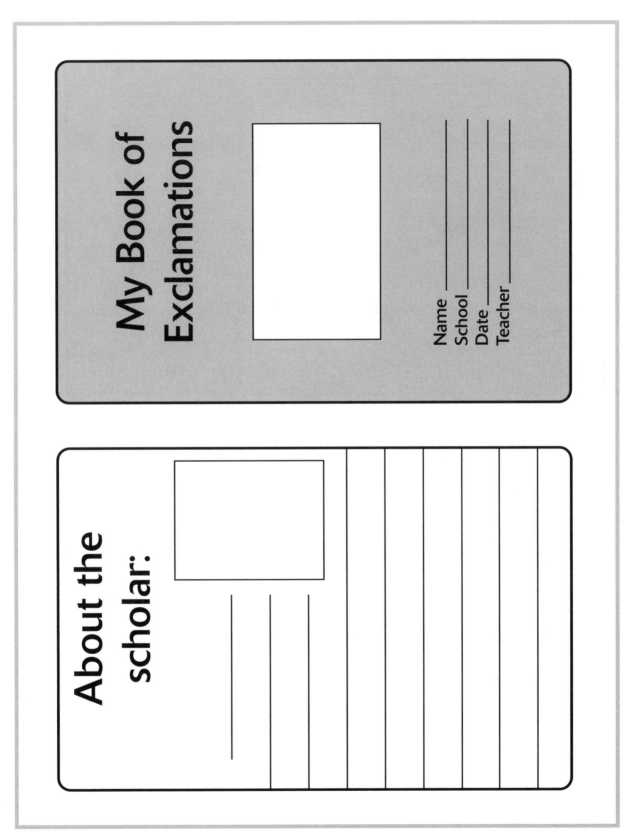

Figure C.9. *My Book of Exclamations.*

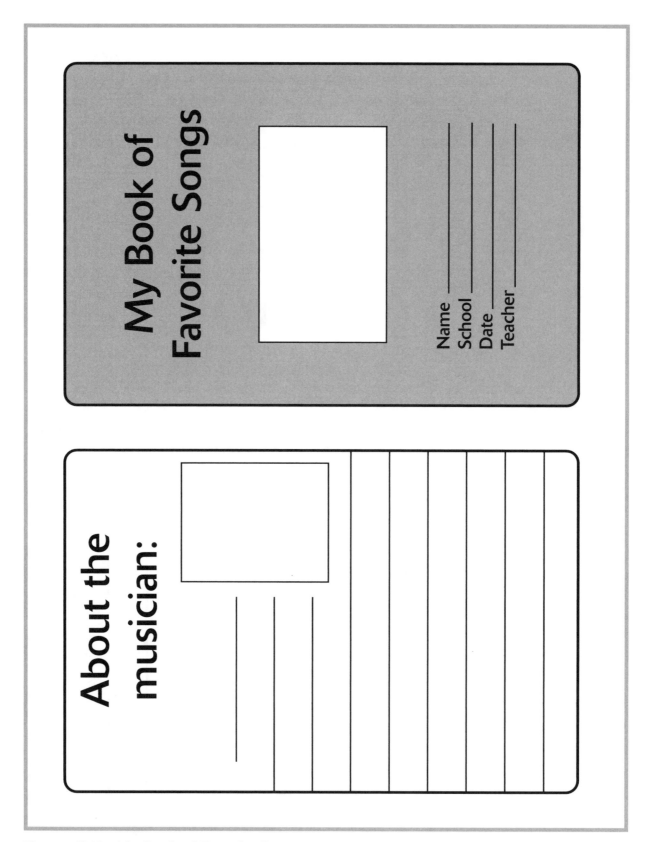

Figure C.10. *My Book of Favorite Songs.*

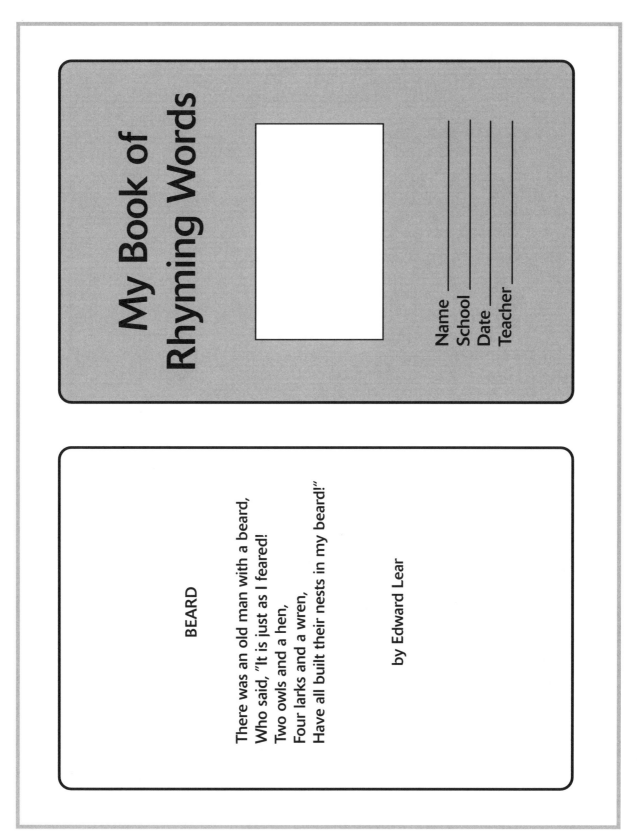

Figure C.11. *My Book of Rhyming Words.*

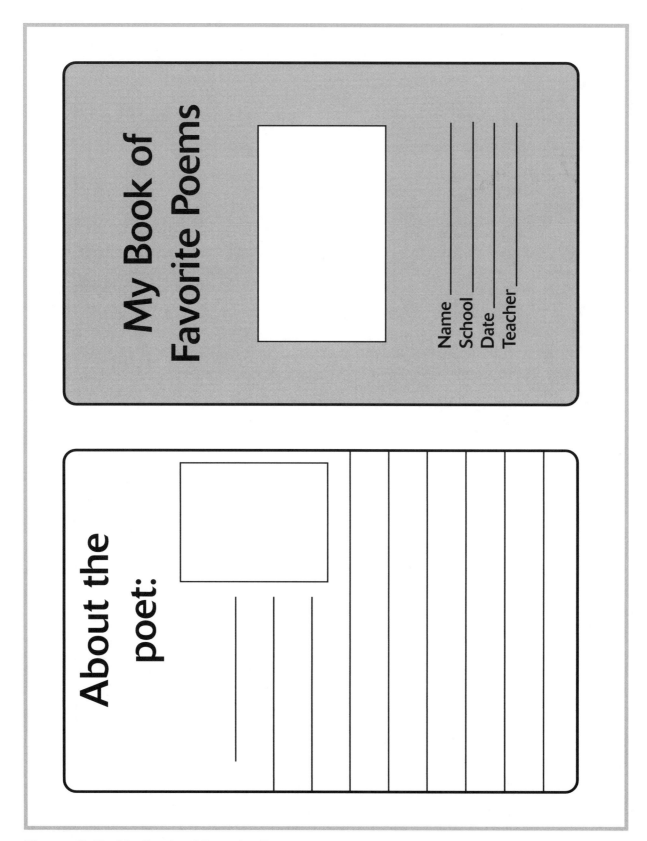

Figure C.12. *My Book of Favorite Poems.*

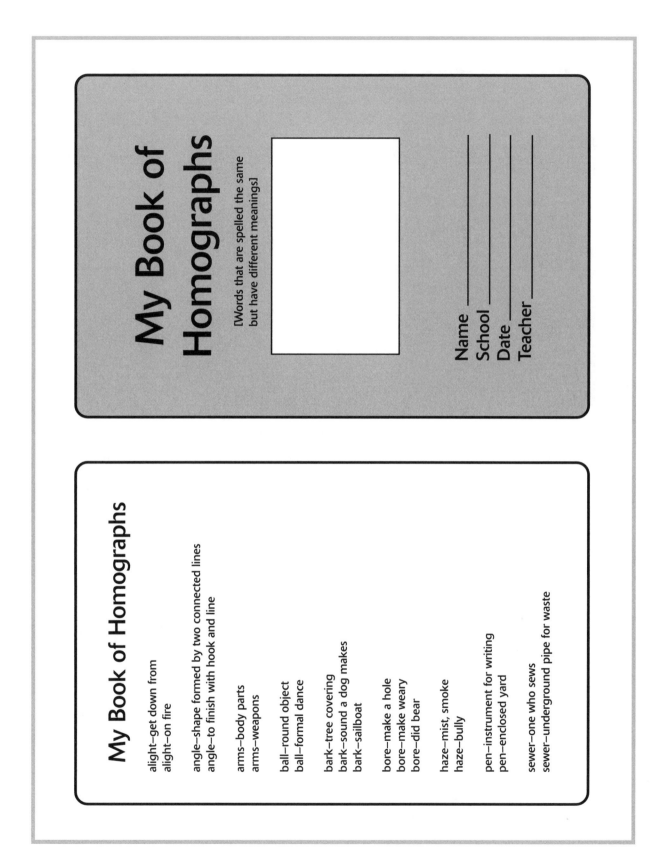

My Book of Homographs

Homographs

[Words that are spelled the same but have different meanings]

Name _____
School _____
Date _____
Teacher _____

My Book of Homographs

alight–get down from
alight–on fire

angle–shape formed by two connected lines
angle–to finish with hook and line

arms–body parts
arms–weapons

ball–round object
ball–formal dance

bark–tree covering
bark–sound a dog makes
bark–sailboat

bore–make a hole
bore–make weary
bore–did bear

haze–mist, smoke
haze–bully

pen–instrument for writing
pen–enclosed yard

sewer–one who sews
sewer–underground pipe for waste

Figure C.13. *My Book of Homographs.*

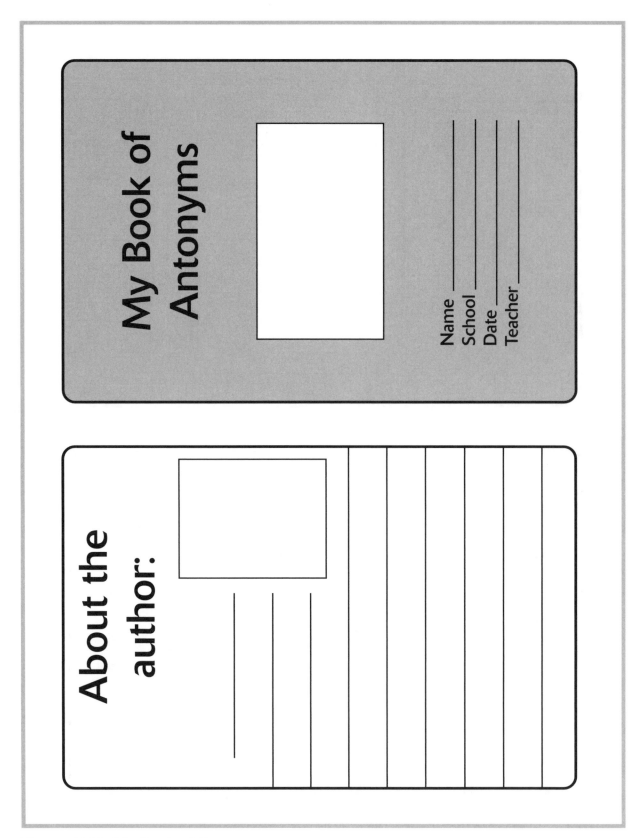

Figure C.14. *My Book of Antonyms.*

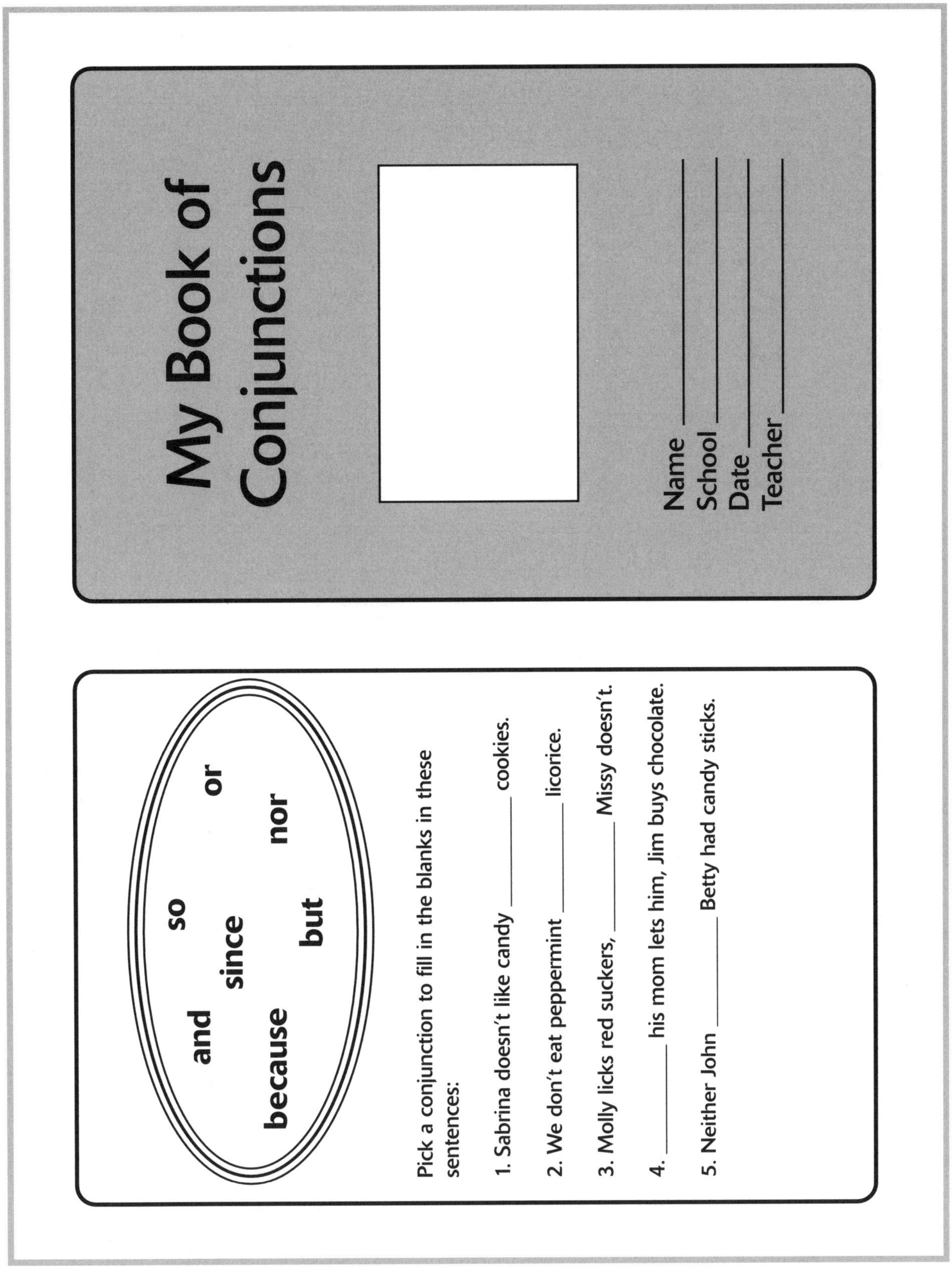

My Book of Conjunctions

Name _____
School _____
Date _____
Teacher _____

and   so   or
since   nor
because   but

Pick a conjunction to fill in the blanks in these sentences:

1. Sabrina doesn't like candy _____ cookies.

2. We don't eat peppermint _____ licorice.

3. Molly licks red suckers, _____ Missy doesn't.

4. _____ his mom lets him, Jim buys chocolate.

5. Neither John _____ Betty had candy sticks.

Figure C.15. *My Book of Conjunctions.*

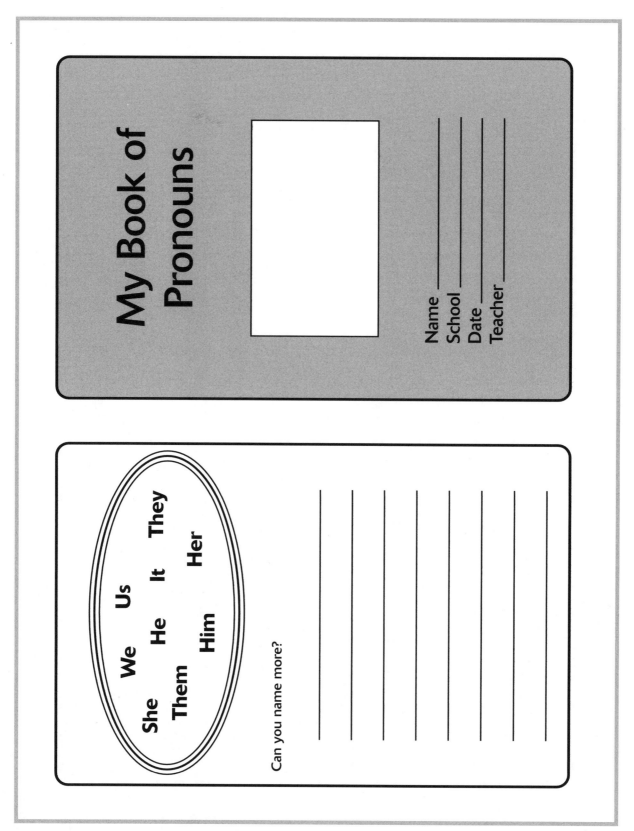

Figure C.16. *My Book of Pronouns.*

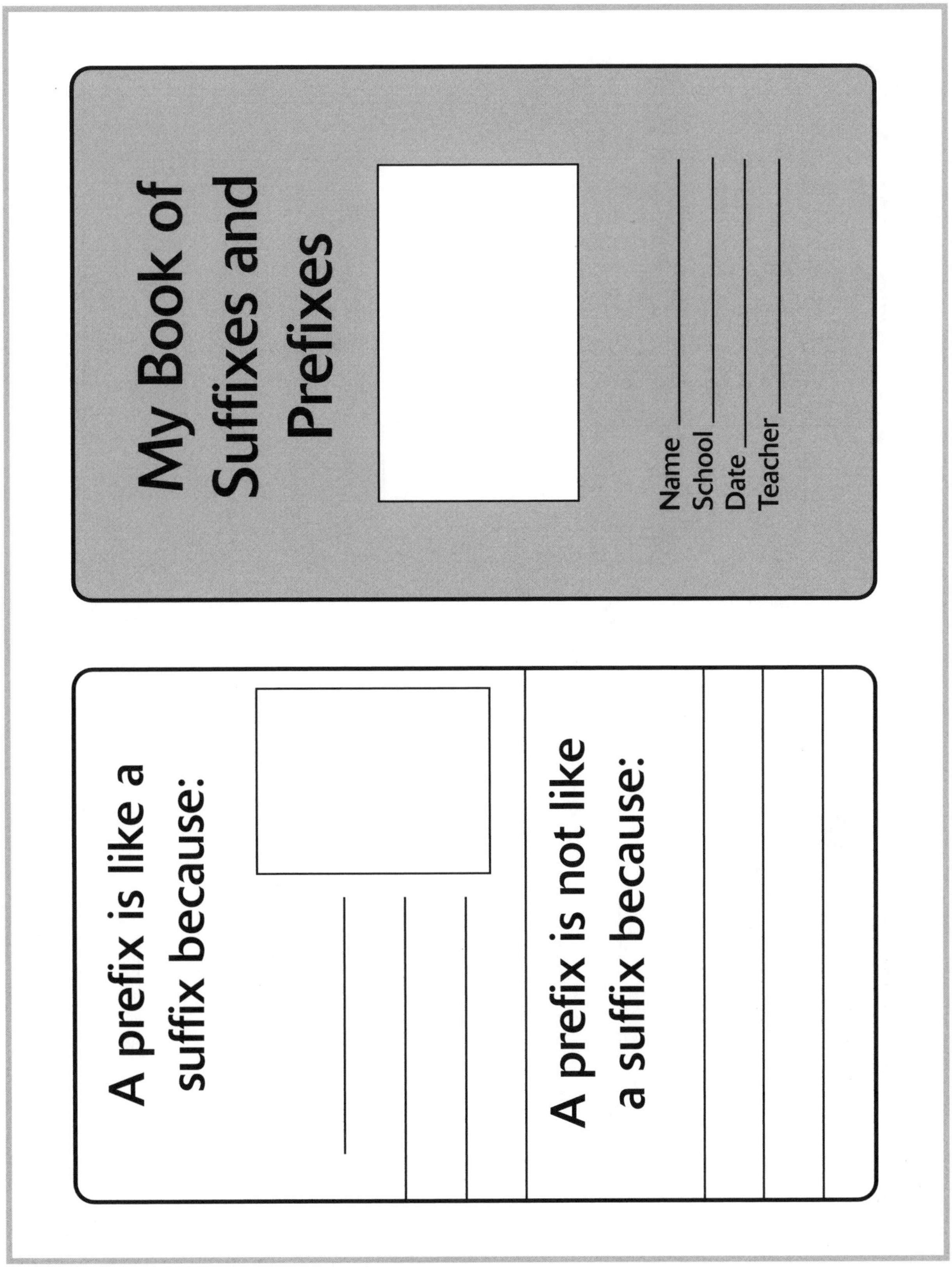

My Book of
Suffixes and
Prefixes

Name
School
Date
Teacher

A prefix is like a
suffix because:

A prefix is not like
a suffix because:

Figure C.17. *My Book of Suffixes and Prefixes.*

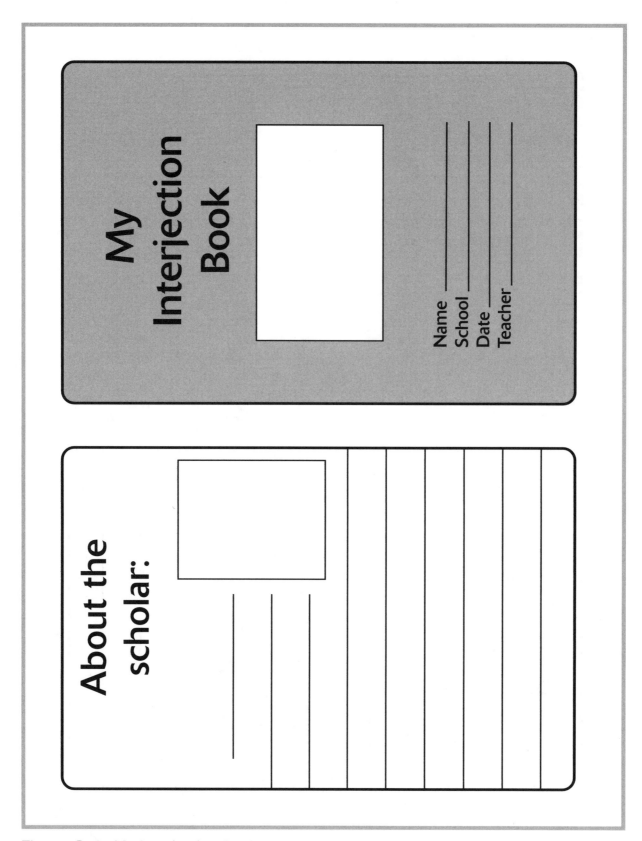

Figure C.18. *My Interjection Book.*

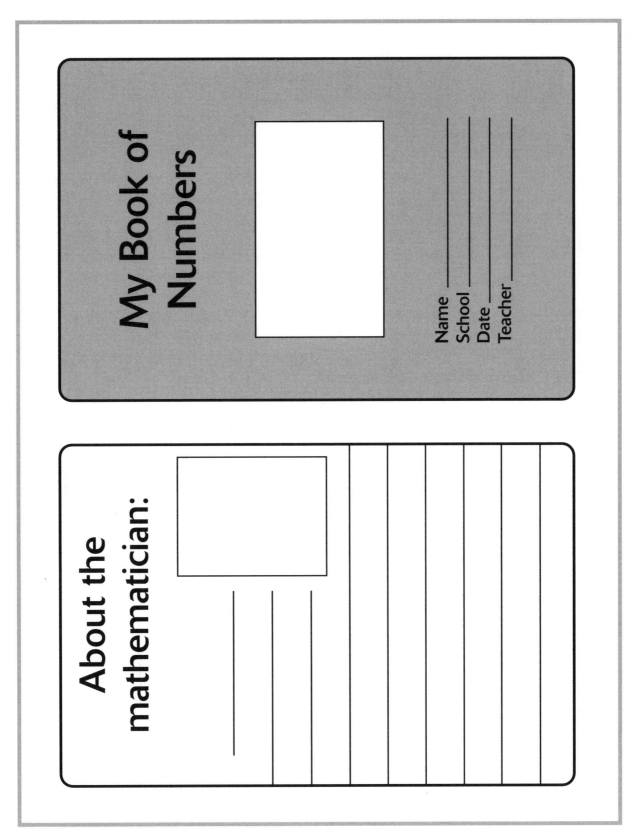

Figure C.19. *My Book of Numbers.*

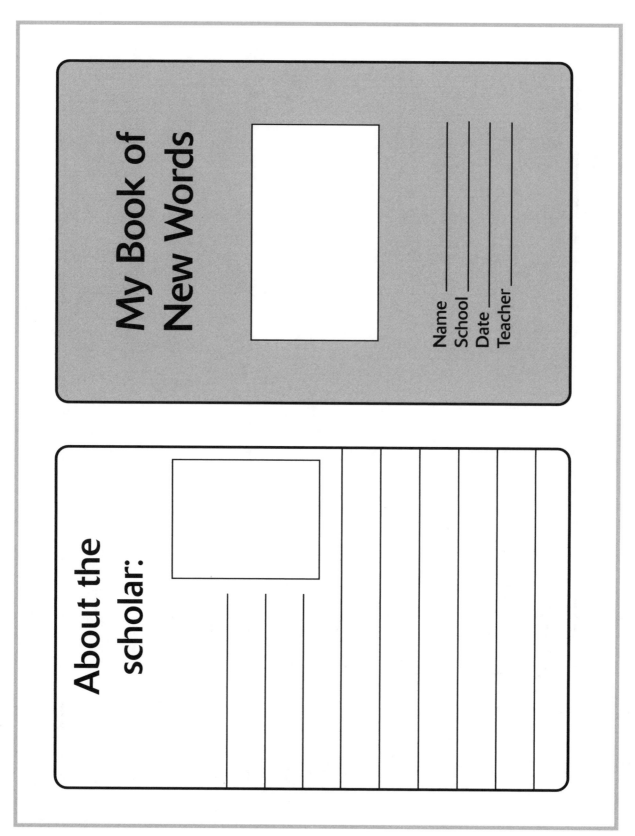

Figure C.20. *My Book of New Words.*

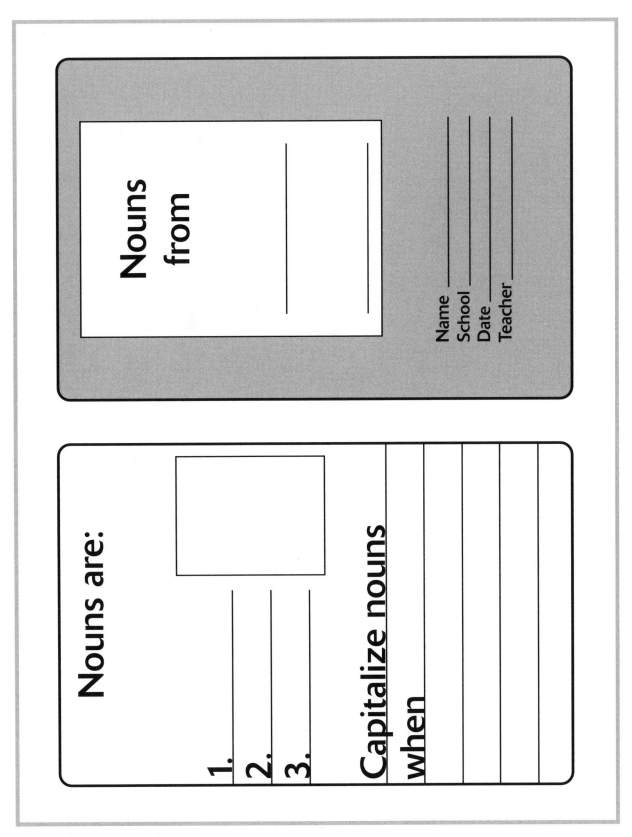

Figure C.21. *Nouns from _____ .*

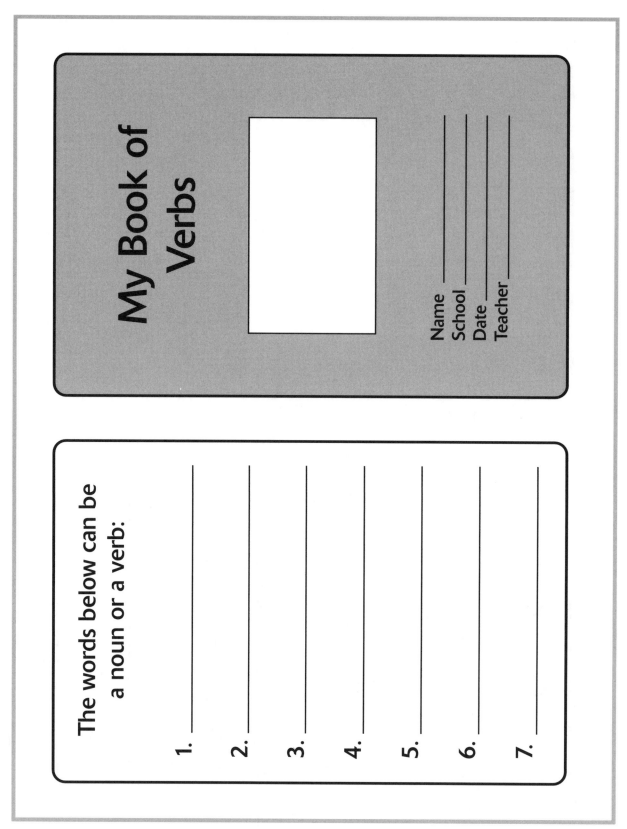

Figure C.22. *My Book of Verbs.*

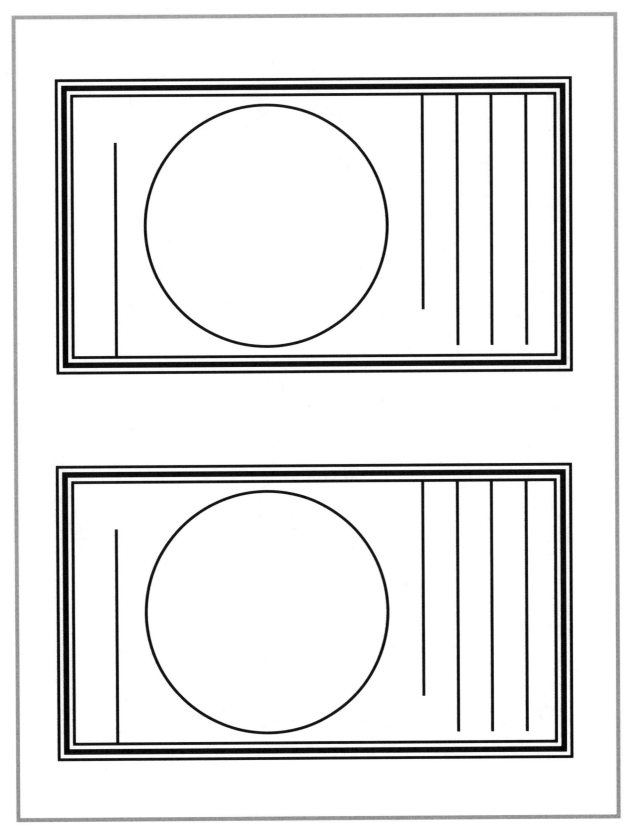

Figure C.23. Master copy of inside pages.

APPENDIX D

Master Pages and Writing Display Ideas

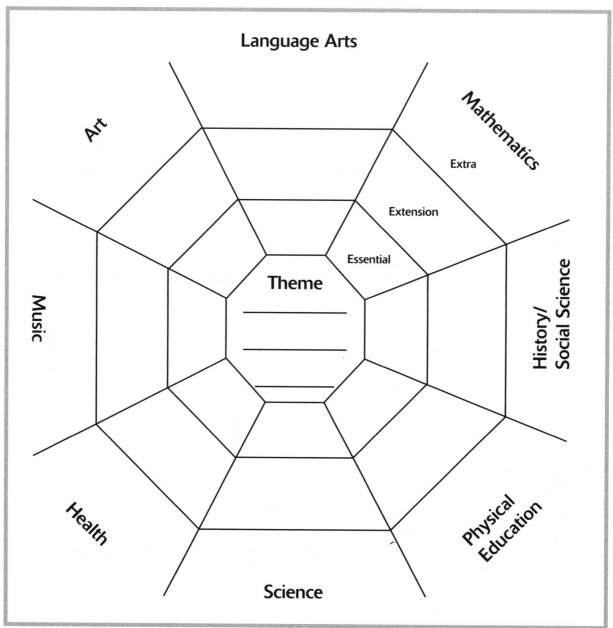

Figure D.1. Unit web master page.

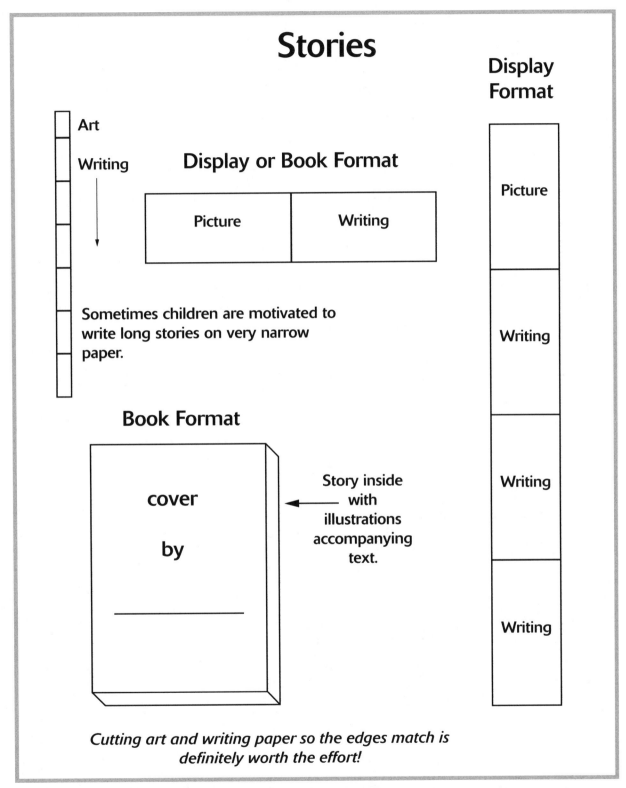

Figure D.2. Writing display ideas (designed by Sandra L. Jenkins, used with permission).

Name _____   Date _____

Math Problem Solving

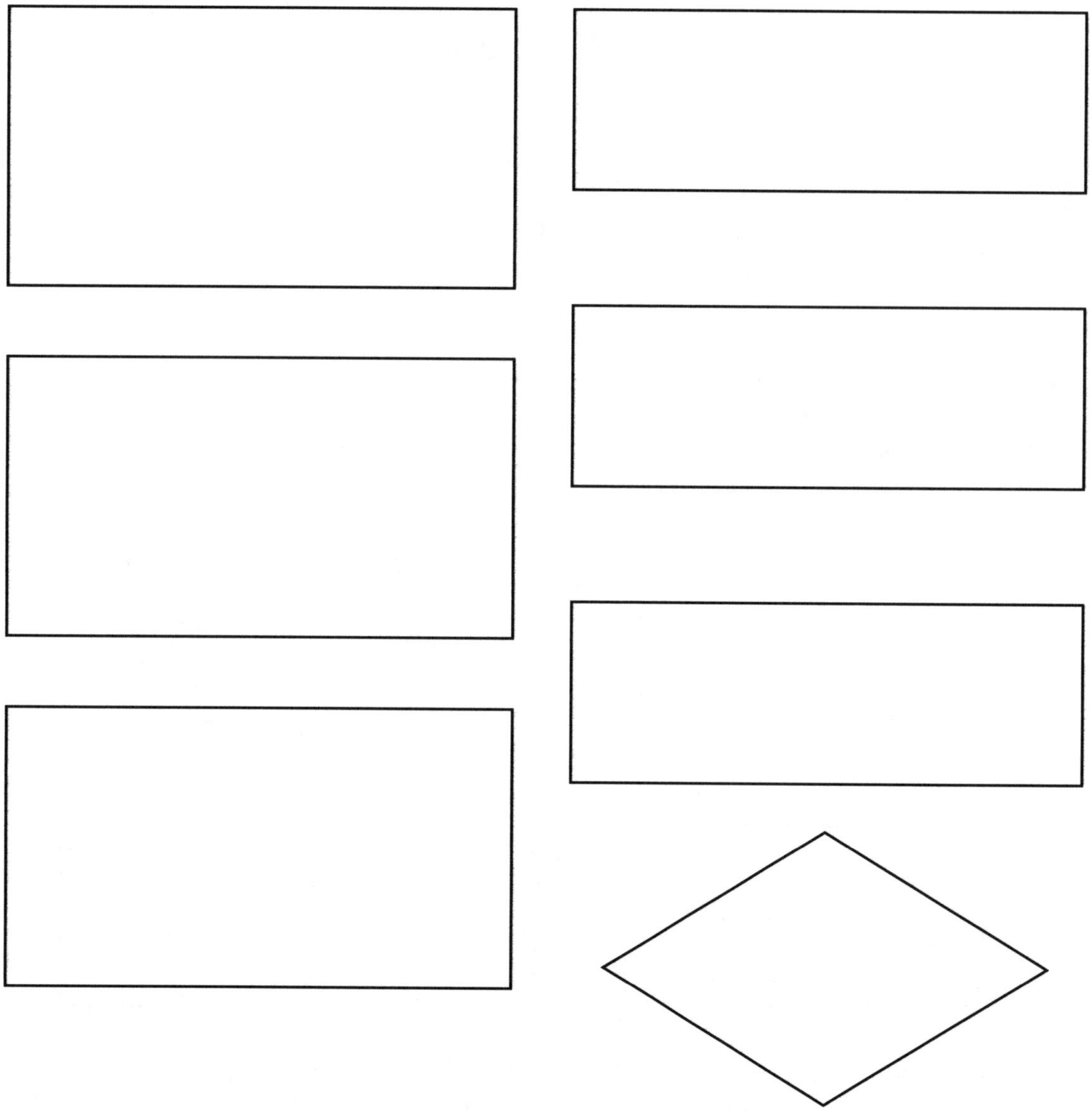

Figure D.3. Math flowchart master.

My ABC Book
of

By: _____

Teacher: _____

School: _____

Date: _____

Figure D.4. *ABC Book* cover.

_____ **is for** _____

Figure D.5. *ABC Book* inside master.

Three Pigs, One Wolf, and Seven Magic Shapes

Original story by Grace Maccarone.
Rewrite designed by Karen Fauss.

Once upon a time three three pigs grew up and left their mama and papa to seek their fortunes. Build and trace a street sign out of the seven tangram pieces. Draw in the setting and add the three little pigs.

Three Pigs, One Wolf, and Seven Magic Shapes

Illustrated with a *new* ending by:

Name _____

School _____

Teacher _____

Room _____

The first pig made a _ _ _ because he was lonely. Build and trace the cat. Draw in the setting.

The first little pig met a magic _ _ _ _ _. He gave him seven magic tangram pieces. Build and trace the magic duck. Draw in the setting.

Build and trace the second little pig using the seven tangram pieces. Draw in the setting.

Big Brad Wolf came running by and _____

Build and trace Big Brad Wolf using the seven tangram pieces.

He gave the pig seven magic tangram pieces.
The pig made a _ _ _ _ _ because he was
frightened. Build and trace the candle. Draw in
the setting.
Along came the wolf and_____

The second little pig met a magic _ _ _ _ _.
Build and trace the rabbit. Draw in the setting.

The swan gave the pig seven magic tangram pieces. The pig made a _ _ _ _ _ because she was wise or smart.
Along came Big Brad Wolf and _____

The third little pig met a magic _ _ _ _. Build and trace the swan. Draw in the setting.

Write about your favorite pig in the story.
My favorite pig was the _____

because _____
_____

But that's not the end of the story.

Now it is your turn to use the seven magic tangram pieces to make a new conclusion or ending to the story. Build and trace your illustration. Draw in the setting.

One day, the pig who built her house out of shapes . . .
_____
_____

My favorite event of the story was when ____
_____
_____
_____

I enjoyed reading this story because ____
_____
_____
_____

Write about the wise or smart choices you
make. For example:

1. I do my best each day.
2. _____
3. _____
4. _____
5. _____
6. _____

References

Bostingl, John Jay. 1996. *Schools of Quality*. Alexandria, VA: Association for Supervision and Curriculum Development.

Byrnes, Margaret A. 1997. *Dr. Deming and His Amazing Quality Idea!* Portales, NM: Pro Que.

Byrnes, Margaret A., Robert A. Cornesky and Lawrence W. Byrnes. 1992. *The Quality Teacher: Implementing Total Quality Management in the Classroom*. Bunnell, FL: Cornesky & Associates.

Byrnes, Margaret A. and Robert A. Cornesky. 1994. *Quality Fusion: Turning Total Quality Management into Classroom Practice*. Port Orange, FL: Cornesky & Associates.

Canfield, Jack and Mark Victor Hansen. 1996. *A 3rd Serving of Chicken Soup for the Soul*. Deerfield Beach, FL: Health Communications.

Dahl, Karin L. and Nancy Farnan. 1998. *Children's Writing: Perspectives from Research*. Newark, DE: International Reading Association.

Faw, Jenny, illustrator. 1996. *A Teacher is a Special Person!* White Plains, NY: Peter Pauper Press.

Garfield, Charles. 1983. *Peak Performers*. New York, NY: Avon Books.

Glasser, William. 1990. *The Quality School*. New York, NY: HarperCollins Publishers.

———. 1993. *The Quality School Teacher*. New York, NY: HarperCollins Publishers.

Gomes, Helio. 1996. *Quality Quotes*. Milwaukee, WI: ASQC Quality Press.

Hartland, Jessie, illustrator. 1999. *Teacher, A Little Book of Appreciation*. Philadelphia, PA: Running Press Book Publishers.

Harvey, Thomas R. and Bonita Drolet. 1994. *Building Teams, Building People*. Lancaster, PA: Technomic Publishing Company.

Jenkins, Lee. 1993. *Applying Quality Principles in Schools*. Cedar Rapids, IA: AASA Total Quality Network in Partnership with Woods Quality Center.

———. 1997. *Improving Student Learning: Applying Deming's Quality Principles in Classrooms*. Milwaukee, WI: ASQ Quality Press.

Jenkins, Sandra. 1990. "Implementing a Literature-Based Language Arts Program for Primary Grades." Masters' thesis, Simpson College, Redding, CA.

McClanahan, Elaine and Carolyn Wicks. 1993. *Future Force: Kids That Want To, Can and Do!* Chino Hills, CA: Pact Publishing.

Rosencrans, Gladys. 1998. *The Spelling Book.* Newark, DE: International Reading Association.

Schmoker, Michael J. 1996. *Results: The Key to Continuous School Improvement.* Alexandria, VA: Association for Supervision and Curriculum Development.

Sitton, Rebecca. 1997. *Rebecca Sitton's Spelling Sourcebook 2.* Scottsdale, AZ: Egger Publishing.

Sowell, Thomas. GOP Lost Because It Wouldn't Speak Out. *Record Searchlight* (Redding, CA), 7 Nov. 1998, sec. A, p.6.

Wong, Harry K. and Rosemary Tripi Wong. 1991. *The First Days of School.* Sunnyvale, CA: Harry K. Wong Publications.

Recommended Resources

Bear, Donald R., Shane Templeton, Marcia Invernizzi and Francine Johnston. 1996. *Words Their Way.* Upper Saddle River, NJ: Prentice Hall.

Bernhardt, Victoria. 1998. *Data Analysis for Comprehensive Schoolwide Improvement.* Larchmont, NY: Eye on Education.

Byrnes, Margaret. 1997. *Quality Tools for Educators.* Portales, NM: Pro Que.

Cornesky, Robert and William Lazarus. 1995. *Continuous Quality Improvement in the Classroom: A Collaborative Approach.* Port Orange, FL: Cornesky & Associates.

Cunningham, Patricia M. and Dorothy P. Hall. 1994. *Making Words.* Carthage, IL: Good Apple, Paramount Publishing.

Ericson, Lita and Moira Fraser Juliebo. 1998. *The Phonological Awareness Handbook for Kindergarten and Primary Teachers.* Newark, DE: International Reading Association.

Schargel, Franklin. 1994. *Transforming Education Through Quality Management.* Princeton, NJ: Eye on Education.

What Works: Research About Teaching and Learning. 1986. Washington, DC: U.S. Department of Education, Government Printing Office.

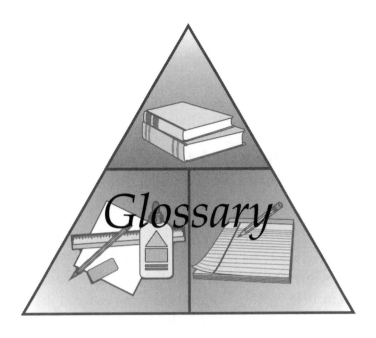

Affinity Diagram a management and planning tool used to organize ideas into natural groupings in a way that stimulates new creative ideas.

aim a concise statement of purpose for the classroom.

ASQ a society for advancing individual and organizational performance excellence worldwide by providing opportunities for learning, quality improvement, and knowledge exchange.

class run chart a graph on which the teacher tracks the progress of the class as a whole or of an individual student.

common cause variation causes that are inherent in any process all the time. A process that has only common causes of variation is said to be stable or predictable.

continuous process improvement includes the actions taken throughout an organization to increase the effectiveness and efficiency of activities and processes in order to provide added benefits to the customer and organization. It is considered a subset of total quality management and operates according to the premise that organizations can always make improvements. Continuous improvement can also be equated with reducing process variation.

customers   students, their parents, the next grade-level staff, and former students.

data   facts presented in descriptive, numeric, or graphic form.

Deming cycle   the Plan-Do-Study-Act cycle. A four-step process for quality improvement. A different way of looking at the scientific method to solve systemic problems in the classroom.

Deming, W. Edwards   a prominent consultant, teacher, and author on the subject of quality. After he shared his expertise in statistical quality control to help the U.S. war effort during World War II, the War Department sent Deming to Japan in 1946 to help that nation recover from its wartime losses. Deming has published more than 200 works, including the well-known books *Quality, Productivity, and Competitive Position* and *Out of the Crisis*. Deming, who developed the 14 points for management, is an ASQC honorary member.

dichotomous key   a way of objectively grading through a series of choices.

epistemology   the study or theory of the origin, nature, methods, and limits of knowledge.

error chart   a chart used by students to keep track of the types of Quality Factors that they are not obtaining in writing assignments and projects.

feedback   comments on success or failure of a particular program from customers.

fishbone diagram   a diagram that illustrates the main causes and subcauses that lead to an effect. The cause-and-effect diagram is one of the seven tools of quality.

flowchart   a graphical representation of the steps in a process. Flowcharts are drawn to better understand processes. The flowchart is one of the seven tools of quality.

force field analysis   a technique for analyzing the forces that aid or hinder an organization in reaching an objective.

histogram   a graphic summary of variation in a set of data. The pictorial nature of the histogram lets people see patterns that are difficult to see in a simple table of numbers. The histogram is one of the seven tools of quality.

information   data transferred into an ordered format that makes them useable and allows one to draw conclusions. In this book, these data are the facts students need to learn during the course of a year.

input   state standards, state standardized tests, the California Reading and Literature Project, district standards, Program Quality Review, expectations of parents, desires of students, special education programs, and student transiency. Each input has negative and positive connotations that impact our class as a system.

knowledge   the ability to use information to create a better future by relating past to current events, problem solving, and experiencing the scientific method.

lower control limit (LCL)   control limit for points below the central line in a control chart.

mentors   those who have been through a given program or experience who help newcomers to the program.

mission statement   an explanation of purpose or reasons for existing as an organization; it provides the focus for the organization and defines its scope of business.

one-hundred-sided die   a special die, containing numbers from one to one hundred, purchased at a school supply or gaming store.

outputs   the results of the year-long learning process.

PDSA Cycle   *see* Deming Cycle.

Plus Delta chart   a way to get feedback from students. It is a simple chart with two columns. One side is the Plus side where students list what they like. The other side is the Delta side where they write the things that need to improve.

process   the students and teacher work together as a team in the classroom to refine and improve the incremental steps in which the concepts are learned and applied. Teaming with other grade levels (higher and lower) also reinforces and enhances their experiences.

process data   data collected each week.

results data   data collected at the end of a school year.

rubric   an objective method of grading performance, often on a scale of one to six.

run chart   a form of trend analysis that uses a graph to show process measurement on the vertical axis against time, with a reference line to show the average of the data. A trend is indicated when a series of collected data points head up or down. In this book, it is a graph used to record test results on which the number correct is the vertical axis and the particular week is the horizontal axis.

scatter diagram   a graphical technique for analyzing the relationship between two variables. Two sets of data are plotted on a graph, with the *y*-axis used for the variable to be predicted and the *x*-axis used for the variable to make the prediction. The graph will show possible relationships (although two variables might appear to be related, they might not be: those who know most about the variables must make that evaluation). The scatter diagram is one of the seven tools of quality. It is used in this book to find how the students are progressing as a class.

self-evaluation form   a form students used to evaluate their daily attitude and behavior.

special cause variation   causes of variation that arise because of special circumstances. They are not an inherent part of a process. Special causes are also referred to as assignable causes. In the classroom, this would be an event outside the normal classroom environment that affects the steady improvement of the class, or of the individual student, as indicated by the run charts.

standard   a statement, specification, or quantity of material against which measured outputs from a process may be judged as acceptable or unacceptable.

supply   the raw materials in the classroom; a teacher's supply consists of all the student's in lower grades before they enter his/her classroom.

system   a network of connecting processes that work together to accomplish the aim.

total quality management (TQM)   a management approach to long-term success through customer satisfaction. It is based upon on the participation of all members of an organization in improving processes.

upper control limits (UCL)   control limit for points above the central line in a control chart.

Weekly Five   The number chosen on the quiz is the square root of the total number of facts that students need to know. The facts are chosen randomly (preview/review) with a hundred-sided die, random numbers list, or Numble Jumble™ on Class Action™.

Weekly Fourteen   The number of spelling words on the weekly quiz is the square root of the total number of words the students need to know. The words are chosen randomly (preview/review) from the first and second hundred high-frequency word lists with a hundred-sided die, random number's list, or Numble Jumble™ on Class Action™.

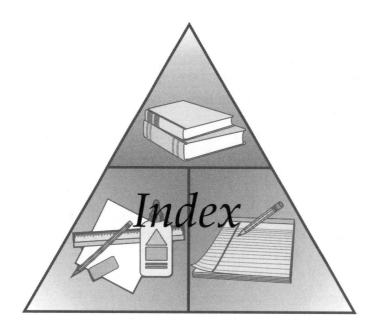

Index